OUTREACH
MINISTRY
VOLUNTEER HANDBOOK

OUTREACH MINISTRY

VOLUNTEER HANDBOOK

Equipping You to Serve

Scripture quotations are taken from the Holy Bible, New International
Version. Copyright © 1973, 1978, 1984, 2011 by Biblica, Inc.®
Used by permission. All rights reserved worldwide.

Scripture quotations marked (ESV) are taken from The ESV® Bible
(The Holy Bible, English Standard Version®) copyright © 2001
by Crossway, a publishing ministry of Good News Publishers.
ESV® Text Edition: 2011. The ESV® text has been reproduced in
cooperation with and by permission of Good News Publishers.

First Edition: Year 2020
Outreach Ministry Volunteer Handbook / Outreach, Inc.
Paperback ISBN: 978-1-951304-30-0
eBook ISBN: 978-1-951304-31-7

CHURCHLEADERS
PRESS

Colorado Springs

OUTREACH MINISTRY

VOLUNTEER HANDBOOK

Equipping You to Serve

Written by
Heather Dunn
Karl Leuthauser
Mark A. Taylor

General Editor
Mark A. Taylor

CHURCHLEADERS
PRESS

Colorado Springs

CONTENTS

FOREWORD

We are his workmanship, created in Christ Jesus for good works,
which God prepared beforehand, that we should walk in them . . .
And he gave the apostles, the prophets, the evangelists, the shepherds
and teachers, to equip the saints for the work of ministry.
—The Apostle Paul (Ephesians 2:10 and 4:11, 12 ESV)

The fact that you are holding this book says some rather encouraging things about you and about your church.

What does it say about you? It suggests that you recognize that the grace and faith that brought you into the kingdom is just the beginning. God has good works prepared for you to do. You play a vital role in the great redemption drama. God's active and seeking love for the world is expressed in you. A book like this can help tune your heart to mission and sharpen your skills. Your interest, and the time you invest reading a book like this, is an encouragement.

What does it say about your church that you are investing time and energy in this resource you are holding? Those who work with you, those who seek to match your skills with ministry opportunities, recognize that the task of the church is not the work of the paid professionals alone. In fact, it is not primarily theirs: it is our work together—all of us. And as we have opportunity to lead and influence others in the church, we make it our aim, as Paul expressed it, "to equip the saints for the work of ministry." A book like this can play a part in that equipping. And it's encouraging whenever a church invests in equipping others for this great work.

As you read, reflect and absorb the wise counsel and good ideas you find here, you will see that your role in the work of the church is vital. The kingdom of God advances as each of us seize the opportunities God places before us and hone our gifts for maximum kingdom impact. For the past two decades, *Outreach* magazine has told the story of people like you and churches like yours sharing the incredibly good news of a God who loves us all self-sacrificingly. It is our privilege to stand in partnership with you and your church as you continue the good work he has begun in your community.

— **@JamesPLong,** Editor
Outreach Magazine
OutreachMagazine.com

INTRODUCTION

to the *Outreach Ministry Guides* Series

Each of you should use whatever gift you have received to serve others, as faithful stewards of God's grace in its various forms (1 Peter 4:10).

$\mathcal{T}$his handbook is part of a series designed to equip and empower church volunteers for effective ministry. If you're reading this, chances are you're a church volunteer. Thanks for your willingness to serve!

Several things make this handbook unique:

- The content is specific and practical for your given area of ministry.
- Experienced ministry practitioners—folks who've worked, served, and helped to train others in this particular area—compiled this information.
- It's written with you—a ministry volunteer— in mind.

Within these pages you'll find three sections. The first gives a brief overview of fundamental principles to provide you with a solid foundation for the ministry area in which you're serving.

Section 2 unpacks various roles and responsibilities. Understanding your role and the roles of your fellow teammates helps the ministry team serve together well.

Finally, Section 3 provides a multitude of practical ministry tools. These ideas and tips will help you demonstrate Jesus' love to the people you serve.

Whether you're a first-time volunteer or a seasoned veteran, my prayer is that the information and practical tools in this handbook will encourage and assist you. May God bless and guide you in your ministry!

— **Matt Lockhart,** Project Manager

INTRODUCTION

to the *Outreach Ministry Volunteer Handbook*

The Son of Man came to seek and to save the lost.
(Luke 19:10)

As the Father has sent me, I am sending you.
(John 20:21)

This book has been created to help you follow the example and continue the work of Jesus today. As you embark on an outreach project chosen by you or organized by your congregation, you are discovering the challenge and the joy of serving in Jesus' name. As you leave the church building and venture into pockets of need nearby, you will meet and know and help others who may not have experienced the love of Jesus before.

Use this handbook as a guide as you prepare to serve. The principles in Section 1 will remind you why your outreach project is so important and help you evaluate next steps. The guidelines in Section 2 will help you figure out where you fit into the worldwide mission of spreading the gospel. And Section 3 will spark your imagination with ideas for reaching every population in dozens of situations. Every outreach-minded Christian will find there a treasure trove of practical help for obeying Christ's command to "Go . . . and make disciples" (Matthew 28:19).

All these possibilities are based on the real-life experience of Christian workers serving a weary and wary world with the hope only Jesus offers. You can join them, emboldened by the fresh strategies and equipped with the remarkable collection of resources you'll find in these pages.

— **Mark A. Taylor,** General Editor

SECTION 1

OUTREACH MINISTRY FOUNDATIONS

CHAPTER 1

OUTREACH 101

*O*utreach. The leader who recruited you said you'd be doing *outreach*. You're glad to help, but it's possible no one ever stopped to define the word for you. You know that *reach* implies some effort, and *out* indicates the project will require some steps beyond yourself. *Out*side. *Out* there. *Out* of my comfort zone? Any of those ideas might fit, but a longer look can clarify what outreach is, and what it is not.

It's NOT about YOU
It IS about THEM

Almost two decades ago Rick Warren wrote a bestseller that started with a phrase most of us have heard since then. "It's not about you," he began in *The Purpose-Driven Life*, and we couldn't choose a better motto to frame our approach to outreach.

It's true, of course, that you are an important element in this enterprise. It wouldn't happen without you and the others on your team. And hopefully you *are* looking forward to the outreach effort you're tackling. It's not wrong to enjoy your service. In fact, it's almost certain you'll find fulfillment in what you do. Jesus said, "It is more blessed to give than to receive" (Acts 20:35), and you should expect to receive many blessings from the outreach you'll offer.

But while you're planning and while you're working, remember to focus on the people you're serving, not your own preferences or comfort or feelings. Hopefully your project planners have done research to discover a real, pressing need your outreach will help to meet, not just a project chosen because the workers will enjoy it.

Outreach is about the people you're serving, so plan on interacting with them if at all possible. Stop to listen. Hear their stories. Make a friend. Offer a warm smile and words of encouragement. And do what they ask—sometimes even when it doesn't make sense to you or it's not what you planned. It's about them. They may even help you. In fact, it's ideal if they will help, because they need the blessing of giving, too. And they know more about their neighborhoods and its needs and preferences than you do. Fold them into your service.

Focus on your team members, too. Be prepared to form relationships that will blossom into friendships and opportunities for all of you to grow. Don't be surprised if some of those working with you are newcomers to your church. Some may barely have attended weekend services. Their desire to serve can grow into an understanding of what motivated you to serve, your commitment to Jesus and longing to demonstrate his love. That leads us to the next point.

It's NOT about YOUR CHURCH
It IS about JESUS

The local church is not the only enterprise planning activities and calling them outreach. Local banks give away ballpoint pens, and coffee shops distribute cup holders at trade shows and malls. But your outreach project is not public relations or marketing for your congregation.

Businesses may call it outreach when they take a day and ask all employees to collect trash, or serve in soup kitchens, or plant flowers outside museums. But your outreach project is about more than doing good deeds.

Your goal is to show the love of Jesus to folks who may not have encountered it before. Your goal is to show how followers of Jesus are not cult-like weirdos seeking new adherents but sold-out followers of the One who died for them. As you serve, remember to love; don't try to sell.

With that in mind, you may or may not choose to advertise your church's name while you're serving. Some churches have forbidden outreach workers to wear T-shirts with the church logo or to drive church vans painted with the church's name. Others say it's OK for a watching world to know that Jesus followers are serving where it's needed most. In a culture that has turned its back on the church, it's good for nonbelievers and those apathetic about Christianity to see Christians serving. Whatever your decision about attaching your church's name to your project, check your motives. The love of Christ compels us to alleviate suffering, provide encouragement, fill empty stomachs, and facilitate healing—even if all that never brings one new person through our church doors.

It's NOT about QUICK CONVERSIONS
It IS about PLANTING SEEDS

Your aim is to live out the love of Jesus and then trust the Holy Spirit to soften hearts and change perspectives of those who see you serve. Trust him to use your project as a link in the chain that eventually pulls them to Christ.

It's possible, of course, that you could meet someone who's ready to hear the gospel and give her life to Christ on the spot. Be ready for that, but don't count on it. Your mission is not to fan out into the community and assault folks who don't know Jesus with promises of eternal damnation. Today more than ever, that approach is more likely to alienate nonbelievers than to attract them.

The time for seeking commitment may come later. Maybe you will make a friend you can see again. Maybe God will use your good will and hard work as one step that leads to their conversion. Pray for that to happen. And while you're serving, make sure nothing in your attitude or conversation gets in the way of the work God wants to do in the hearts of those you're serving.

Jesus promised that lifting him up would draw people to him (John 12:32). Lift him up and believe he will use your work to accomplish his will.

It's NOT just about SERVICE
It IS about MAKING DISCIPLES

But while you're thinking about all of that, remember this final word. The purpose of outreach is to make disciples of Jesus Christ. Some who see you serve will think differently about the church and be willing someday to take a second look at Jesus. Some who serve with you will discover new reasons and opportunities to seek him more diligently. Your project can open the door to relationships that will drive people deeper into Scripture and closer to those who live by it.

That's your goal. It's the most important goal in the world. And God will use you to make it happen right where you live today.

CHAPTER 2

5 PRINCIPLES FOR EFFECTIVE OUTREACH

*N*ever in our lifetimes has there been a greater need for outreach. Research shows the percentage of our population attending church on any weekend is declining. And the number of those claiming no affiliation with any institutional religion continues to grow. And yet many are looking for answers to life's deepest questions; many seek spiritual meaning beyond their physical existence.

Reaching seekers today demands a fresh approach and a renewed commitment to reaching them.

Some reading this book will remember a day when all our energy was spent on creating better programs to attract more people to our church building. But no matter what we did, many in our culture have paid no attention.

Some of us have given great attention to theories and principles of church growth. But much of that emphasis simply resulted in creating congregations more attractive to Christians who were dissatisfied with the congregation they previously attended.

Some of us have felt that faithfulness should be our goal. So we have given our money, attended the services, read daily devotions, and joined small groups. But much of that activity has turned our focus inward. Our friends, our church, our youth ministry, our children's program, our women's ministry, our music—it's all so good, it's all so wholesome, everyone there is so nice, it's a wonderful shelter from the evil around us. But as we've isolated ourselves from the world, more and more of the world has headed for Hell.

Some of us, remembering that the mission of Jesus is to seek and save the lost (Luke 19:10) have made drastic changes in our church programming to attract people who don't know him. Modern music accompanied by fog machines and lasers, practical electives, a contemporary approach to preaching, worship services at times besides Sunday morning. And some of us have even created church staff positions called "outreach pastor." None of that—absolutely none of that—is wrong or bad. Of course the church must change with the times.

But the church does not exist for itself. The need of the day and the truth of Scripture demand that we realize this: the church does not have a mission; God's mission has the church. Now is the time to reach out. Now is the time to engage the world on its turf instead of assuming they'll meet us on ours. If we do not realize that, if we do not reach out to those who have not joined us, we become consumers in a club. Sadly, the club mentality is under the surface of many church initiatives and buried in the psyche of many Christians.

But those reading this book can change that.

We can acknowledge that God is a missionary God, and we can recapture our missionary identity. We've long supported foreign missionaries who have left the comfort of the familiar to enter different cultures with God's good news. They have learned new languages and discovered needs in South American jungles or the African bush or teeming cities in Asia or Europe. They have obeyed the command of Jesus to go and make disciples (Matthew 28:19).

This handbook is full of strategies and ideas to help us do that where we live. Some of this outreach, maybe most of it at first, will be organized by church leaders. God bless them! But we can pray for more. We can ask God to kindle a heart for the lost, a missionary spirit and identity, inside every Christian. Outreach may begin with plans inside a church office, but it must grow from the passion of every Christian in every neighborhood.

The outreach needed today has several important characteristics. We can think about them using a simple acrostic based on the word *REACH*.

R = Relational
Effective outreach makes connections with people.

The project is not the point; the people are our purpose. We may stage impressive programs or do remarkable work. But if we have built no relationship with anyone outside our group, we've succeeded at public relations more than outreach.

Effective outreach mobilizes Christians to hear the stories of the people they're serving. People are longing for someone to listen to them. They will remember that Christians took time to pay attention to their need. It's so much easier to paint a wall than to sit down with someone we're serving and just let them talk. But when we look at people and listen to them, we're following the example of Jesus.

Some like the word *incarnational* to describe this strategy. Jesus was God *incarnated*. He took on flesh and blood and bones to demonstrate the purposes and priorities of God. With our outreach, we have a similar opportunity to show what the love of Jesus looks like.

When we look at the example of Jesus, we see him again and again interacting with the people around him. He did not do his good works at a distance from the crowd. He mingled with people. He touched and listened. He laughed and ate. He had supernatural ability to see into the hearts of people and to perceive their need. We can pray for the Holy Spirit to make us similarly aware as we serve people on playgrounds, in schools, at shelters, or raking leaves on their front lawns.

"But I'm an introvert," some will respond. "Extending myself to others is hard work for me." We can encourage these folks to relax, pray for the right opportunity, and try. Sooner or later they will meet someone else who's shy or quiet or alone. Or they may discover an extrovert hungry for someone to hear them talk! With God's help, introverts will be surprised at how effective they can be—and how fun and meaningful it can be to build relationships.

And remember that outreach initiatives build relationships among workers as well as with those being served. A local congregation's commitment to outreach can attract many who are craving connections and looking for meaningful ways to get outside themselves. Many around us, especially young adults, are seeking causes to give themselves to. When the church spends its resources to meet real needs in its community, it attracts people who are more interested in changing the world than supporting an institution.

The wise outreach leader encourages anyone and everyone to participate. It's true, of course, that a non-Christian won't be sharing the love of Christ, at least not intentionally. But he will experience this love as he sees how the Christians around him are serving. He will feel it as they demonstrate their love for him.

E = Evangelistic
Effective outreach seeks to make disciples of Christ.

Here's the tension outreach leaders experience: Our purpose is to bring people to Jesus. But if we simply go door-to-door distributing tracts, we'll probably be wasting our time. If we buttonhole people on the sidewalk or preach with a megaphone from street corners, we'll likely do more harm than good for the cause of Christ. And if we accost schoolteachers or soup kitchen guests or nursing home residents with a gospel presentation every time we serve them, they may ask us to quit coming.

So, how do outreach projects lead to making disciples? There are several answers.

• Service is our best apologetic.

There was a time when leading unbelievers to Jesus was mainly a rational issue. Show them the Bible is true. Tell why it's reasonable to believe in God. List the proofs that Jesus is God's Son. Repeat the Scriptures explaining how to become a Christian.

We may still have the chance for such conversations. It's still important to know and believe and be able to explain the truth about God. But something else must come first if we're to turn the heads of many who completely ignore the church. (It's not that they don't believe the claims of

Christianity; they haven't stopped to consider them.) In a culture where many think the church is irrelevant, our outreach creates the chance to show that's not true.

• Service sets the stage for more influence later.

Listen to the testimonies of leaders whose churches are active with outreach:

"One way we reach non-Christians is because we have an excellent reputation in the community. Again and again we hear, 'We came because there's a buzz about this church in this town.'"

"Seeing us out serving is not going to make someone a disciple. But when that person has a need, they think of us first."

"We believe the more we can do to winsomely represent Jesus in a beautiful way, the sooner they'll come to us when they experience crisis in their lives."

• Service helps Christians become like Jesus.

Jesus called fishermen to follow him and become fishers for people (Matthew 4:19). People were his reason for living. He cared more for lost people than anyone else who's walked our planet. Watch him interact with the woman at the well (John 4:1-26), with Zacchaeus (Luke 19:1-10), with the woman caught in adultery (John 8:1-11), with the rich young ruler (Matthew 19:16-22)—the examples go on and on. We are following his example when we care about people the way Jesus did, when our goal above every priority and any concern is to make disciples. With our commitment to outreach we are demonstrating the best definition of Christian maturity.

• Service can point servants to Christ, too.

As we welcome non-Christians to join us in outreach, we create an atmosphere that may point them to Christ. As we include non-Christians in our projects, we should be ready someday to talk with them about their own faith. While we're praying for those we'll meet and serve, we can also remember to pray for those serving with us, especially for those whose understanding of God is small. They offer a great opportunity for evangelism.

A = Assertive

Effective outreach is intentional.

Effective outreach is not a program, but a posture. The commitment to disciple-making dominates every decision, every budget and staffing discussion, every calendar-planning session. Several specific tactics support that strategy.

• Discover needs.

The 121 outreach ideas presented in this book (Chapter 7) offer many outreach possibilities. However, choosing one of those ideas may not be the best place to start. The better beginning point is with an investigation of the surrounding community.

Effective outreach goes to those outside the church and in the community to ask, "What do you need?" We may be surprised at the answer. Something as simple as refreshments for a monthly community meeting could be a good start. Jesus said he who is faithful with little will be entrusted with more (see Luke 19:12-26). When we prove ourselves reliable and unselfish, others will see they can count on us, and our opportunities to serve will grow.

Talk to the mayor, the police department, a public school principal or school board member, the town council, the manager of a senior citizens residence, and any community task force or nonprofit agency seeking to solve problems where you live. All of them are understaffed. All of them are juggling competing priorities with a limited budget. All of them need help.

As you sort through the needs you're finding, choose among them keeping three questions in mind: (1) Is this consistent with God's will? (2) How pressing is the need? (3) Do we have the resources to help?

• **Form partnerships.**

Be willing humbly to take the role of a servant. Not every initiative can or should be started by a local congregation. A church's outreach workers don't need to be singled out or publicized as they join others already serving. One congregation follows this philosophy as it interacts with its community: "You can do it. We can help."

Sometimes it's productive for several congregations to partner together to address a pressing problem. But effective outreach does not begin by copying or reproducing what another church is doing. Concerned citizens who may not know Christ are trying to create a better world. Let's start by listening to them first.

• **Decentralize the task.**

To reach an increasingly secular culture, local churches must find ways to create missionaries of every member. Throughout history the church has grown like wildfire when scores of individual Christians have burned with fervor to share the good news.

One way to do this is through a congregation's small groups. One church challenged every small group to choose a mission beyond just meeting to study the Bible. Another church gave $1,000 to each small group with the charge to use the funds to serve others. Another divided its annual marketing budget among small groups to use for outreach.

One church converted a food truck into a mobile outreach van. Any group of church members can use it for whatever project the group chooses. The group members create the project, buy gas for the van, and pay for any giveaways. Church leaders regularly receive thanks for a group's good deeds when the leaders had no idea what the group was doing.

Jesus gave his Great Commission (Matthew 28:18-20) to individuals, not an institution. Effective outreach today happens when the local church is a facilitator, not a bottleneck.

Our prayer for those reading this book is that they will find many ways to reach out without waiting for their congregation to give them permission or even funding. Outreach is every Christian's priority.

C = Calm
Effective outreach grows from patient trust in God.

While we remember that our purpose is to evangelize, we can also trust the Lord of the harvest (Matthew 9:38) to do his work. Paul the apostle made this clear when he wrote the church in Corinth:

> *I planted the seed, Apollos watered it, but God has been making it grow. So neither the one who plants nor the one who waters is anything, but only God,*

who makes things grow. The one who plants and the one who waters have one purpose, and they will each be rewarded according to their own labor. For we are co-workers in God's service; you are God's field, God's building. (1 Corinthians 3:6-9)

Each act of service we perform can be a link in the chain that draws others to Christ. We can serve joyfully without demanding that God show us how he'll use our work. We can trust the Holy Spirit to combine our influence with that of others eventually to soften the heart of the unbeliever.

Sometimes we may feel the Spirit working in the current moment. Those in need will almost always be open to prayer. And we may sense they'd listen if we shared the hope Jesus gives us.

But it's best not to force this. Effective outreach stays calm. Effective outreach remembers what Paul said, "God makes things grow." The Lord asks us first to create an atmosphere that will allow his love to take root.

H = Heart
Effective outreach grows from hearts submitted to God.

Our passion for reaching the lost is the fuel that drives our efforts. Volunteers sign up for outreach projects with many motives, and we're glad if they get something back from what they're giving. But effective outreach flourishes as Christians resist the natural tendency to satisfy self.

Constantly we counter the flesh to give and serve and do. It's almost never convenient. The flesh will tug to the very end. Effective outreach challenges Christians to love beyond themselves. Effective outreach remembers the promise of Jesus: "Whoever wants to save their life will lose it, but whoever loses their life for me and for the gospel will save it" (Mark 8:35).

Effective outreach may begin with a Saturday afternoon or a weekday morning devoted to service. But its ultimate goal is to help Christians sacrifice self for the sake of Christ every day, and doing so while keeping in mind this admonishment from the apostle Peter:

> *But in your hearts revere Christ as Lord. Always be prepared to give an answer to everyone who asks you to give the reason for the hope that you have. But do this with gentleness and respect.* (1 Peter 3:15)

CHAPTER 3

THE SCRIPTURAL BASIS FOR OUTREACH

*Y*ou'll find many of these Scriptures referenced elsewhere in this handbook. But here, for easy reading, is a compelling list of Bible passages that show why God is concerned about outreach.

You may decide to use these to prepare your heart for your outreach project. Meditate on the verses. Consider the thoughts and questions after each one. Choose one or two of these to memorize and repeat to yourself in the days before your project.

You might decide to discuss some of these with your whole group or choose one to read aloud as you gather on the day of your project.

Genesis 12:1-3

> *The LORD had said to Abram, "Go from your country, your people and your father's household to the land I will show you. I will make you into a great nation, and I will bless you; I will make your name great, and you will be a blessing."*

Throughout the Bible we see that God is a missionary God. God blessed Abram to be a blessing. How can you share the blessings God has given you with those you know and those you'll serve?

Mark 1:16-18

As Jesus walked beside the Sea of Galilee, he saw Simon and his brother Andrew casting a net into the lake, for they were fishermen. "Come, follow me," Jesus said, "and I will send you out to fish for people." At once they left their nets and followed him.

Who first encouraged you to follow Jesus? How has that invitation changed your life? How could that invitation change lives among those you'll serve?

Mark 8:35

For whoever wants to save their life will lose it, but whoever loses their life for me and for the gospel will save it.

Have you ever experienced saving your life by losing it for God? Thank him for your opportunity to "lose your life for the gospel" by participating in your outreach project.

Mark 10:42-45

Jesus called them together and said, "You know that those who are regarded as rulers of the Gentiles lord it over them, and their high officials exercise authority over them. Not so with you. Instead, whoever wants to become great among you must be your servant, and whoever wants to be first must be slave of all. For even the Son of Man did not come to be served, but to serve, and to give his life as a ransom for many."

How does thinking of yourself as a slave affect your attitude toward your outreach project? How does imagining Jesus by your side as you serve motivate you?

Luke 14:21-23

Then the owner of the house became angry and ordered his servant, "Go out quickly into the streets and alleys of the town and bring in the poor, the crippled, the blind and the lame."

"Sir," the servant said, "what you ordered has been done, but there is still room."

Then the master told his servant, "Go out to the roads and country lanes and compel them to come in, so that my house will be full."

Read Luke 14:15-23 to see the context for the above quote. What does this parable teach us about the feelings of Jesus toward society's outcasts?

Luke 15:2

This man welcomes sinners and eats with them.

Read all of Luke 15 to remind yourself how and why Jesus wants his followers to reach out to those who don't know him. What do the attitudes and actions of those in the parables tell you about how we should feel and what we should do? What can we learn from Jesus who regularly put himself in close contact with sinners?

Luke 19:10

For the Son of Man came to seek and to save the lost.

How much of your time and attention is given to those who don't know Jesus? How intentional have you been to "seek" them for his sake? How does your church's outreach ministry align with the purposes of Jesus as he stated them in this passage?

John 13:12-17

When he had finished washing their feet, he put on his clothes and returned to his place. "Do you understand what I have done for you?" he asked them. "You call me 'Teacher' and 'Lord,' and rightly so, for that is what I am. Now that I, your Lord and Teacher, have washed your feet, you also should wash one another's feet. I have set you an example that you should do as I have done for you. Very truly I tell you, no servant is greater than his master, nor is a messenger greater than the one who sent him. Now that you know these things, you will be blessed if you do them."

Foot washing was a humble, dirty task in Jesus' time. What activities in your outreach project could be described in the same way? How do these words of Jesus motivate and encourage you as you anticipate your project?

John 20:21

As the Father has sent me, I am sending you.

How does it help you to believe you're being sent into service not just by your congregation, but also by Jesus himself?

2 Corinthians 5:14-15

For Christ's love compels us, because we are convinced that one died for all, and therefore all died. And he died for all, that those who live should no longer live for themselves but for him who died for them and was raised again.

When did you decide that living for Jesus also included reaching out to those who don't know him? Why is it important to you to get beyond your circle of Christian friends to find ways to express your faith?

Matthew 28:16-20

Then the eleven disciples went to Galilee, to the mountain where Jesus had told them to go. When they saw him, they worshiped him; but some doubted. Then Jesus came to them and said, "All authority in heaven and on earth has been given to me. Therefore go and make disciples of all nations, baptizing them in the name of the Father and of the Son and of the Holy Spirit, and teaching them to obey everything I have commanded you. And surely I am with you always, to the very end of the age."

What does Jesus say about himself in this passage? What does he tell his followers to do? What does he promise them if they'll obey him? Which section of this passage encourages you most as you anticipate serving?

John 3:16

> *For God so loved the world that he gave his one and only Son, that whoever believes in him shall not perish but have eternal life.*

With all the physical preparations you're making for your project, think about its potential to make a difference beyond this year and your place. What impact for eternity are you hoping to help make?

Ephesians 4:11-13

> *So Christ himself gave the apostles, the prophets, the evangelists, the pastors and teachers, to equip his people for works of service, so that the body of Christ may be built up until we all reach unity in the faith and in the knowledge of the Son of God and become mature, attaining to the whole measure of the fullness of Christ.*

What is the means for bringing Christians to maturity? How have you been equipped for works of service? How could you equip someone else?

Philippians 2:3

> *Do nothing out of selfish ambition or vain conceit. Rather, in humility value others above yourselves.*

Read Philippians 2:1-11 to see this verse in context. What does this passage teach you about the spirit in which you should serve? What does it remind you about the attitudes you should adopt toward those who will serve with you?

CHAPTER 4

WHAT HAPPENS WHEN CHRIST FOLLOWERS REACH OUT

As we've researched and compiled this book, we've come across several stories showing the impact of an individual Christian committed to intentionally taking good news to those who don't know it.
Read the following examples and then ask yourself:
Do I have a story like this I could tell?
What would it mean to me—and to God—if my influence had an impact like this?

*G*len, a pastor in Tucson, Arizona, agreed to do a neighborhood cleanup project with some other guys. Helping them were several fellows who had never connected with a local church. "That's the advantage of a project like this," Glen says. "You get to rub shoulders with people you'd never see first inside your building."

He doesn't remember the whole conversation he had with Alex, one of his co-workers on the project, but he does remember what Alex said toward the end of the workday. Recently retired, Alex told Glen he had just started reading the Bible—and he found the whole thing terribly confusing.

"Would you like to study the Bible together?" Glen asked. And Alex was eager to take him up on the offer.

Glen chose a simple Bible-study tool based on the Discovery Bible Study approach used widely in world missions. Several variations of this method can be found online. They involve a series of simple questions virtually anyone can use. At Pantano Christian Church where Glen ministers, the pattern is to read a text and then discuss answers to three questions: What happened? What does the text tell me about me, God, and the world? What am I going to do about it?

Glen has met with Alex to study the Bible every week for a year. Alex has found faith, but he's still not comfortable coming to church. So Glen invited him to watch their worship online, and he has agreed. Alex has been talking with his friends about the experience.

"The Word of God and the work of the Holy Spirit combine to touch the hearts of those who read the Bible using this approach," Glen says. "I believe this is a picture of how we're going to win those in our post-Christian culture to Christ."

Colin and Jake were great friends in college. Colin was a Christian, but Jake was not. After graduation Colin decided intentionally to stay in touch with his school buddies, for the sake of Christ. He and Jake did all the things they'd enjoyed in school: hiking, kayaking, sports. Jake was not particularly open to faith, but Colin remained his friend. After a couple of years, Jake had a major health scare, so serious that his wife was afraid he would die. She'd had passing contact with the church, and she asked Colin if he and the church would pray for Jake. At one point they weren't sure he'd live through the night.

But he did. Throughout his ordeal, Colin visited him in the hospital, cut his grass, and demonstrated a level of compassion and care that was more than the concern of an old college buddy. Members of the church, motivated by the missional culture created at the church, reached out to Jake and his wife. His illness made him rethink life. His Christian friends were ready to share hope as well as help. About a year after he fell ill, Jake was baptized.

Dave Dummitt has many stories about the spontaneous outreach activities of groups from the congregation he founded and where he served for 15 years, 2/42 Community Church in Brighton, Michigan. One group decided to distribute cups of hot chocolate to shoppers lined up outside a shopping center at 3:00 a.m. on a cold Black Friday morning. Group members had purchased everything for the project, including the mugs with the caption, "You've Been Mugged by 2/42 Church." He especially remembers one person who decided to visit the congregation after receiving the chocolate. Soon this fellow became a Christian, and then a group leader, and eventually a part-time paid staff member in the church's children's ministry. Now he serves as the congregation's full-time executive minister, and it all started with the passion for outreach from a group of everyday Christians.

Francis Collins, director of the National Institute of Health, was an atheist as a third-year medical student in North Carolina. Sitting at the bedside with people of faith forced him to reconsider his assumptions about God. He remembers one patient in particular who explained that her faith in Jesus gave her the strength to endure the suffering she was experiencing. When she asked him about *his* faith, he realized he could not ignore her question. Later he became friends with a minister who patiently heard his objections and listened to his questions and eventually introduced him to *Mere Christianity* by C.S. Lewis. Finally, at age 27 he became a Christian; it all started with the simple question of a faithful witness who was as interested in his faith as her own problem. [1]

---

1   You can read more about Collins in Peter Wehner's interview with him, posted by *The Atlantic* at https://bit.ly/2xwZt3a.

SECTION 2

THE OUTREACH MINISTRY TEAM

CHAPTER 5

OUTREACH MINISTRY
OPPORTUNITIES AND ROLES

The Secret Formula

*I*f there is a secret formula to outreach, you'll find it in Acts 17. When Paul stood up at the Areopagus in Athens, he complimented the people of Athens on their devotion to religion. Then he used their statue to an unknown god to begin talking about the One True God. As a result of his explanation, some sneered, some became curious, and others believed—including Damaris and Dionysius. Of course, the belief and the transformation came from the work of the Holy Spirit undergirding and guiding Paul's words. But Paul's method shows a foundational principle of all effective outreach. Simply put, he built a bridge.

Paul certainly could not have been pleased to see the rampant idolatry in Athens. As he walked around the justice center of the city, he must have been dismayed or even angry at the false worship that often led to licentiousness. But not only did Paul refrain from attacking and criticizing their idolatry, he used it as a launching point to teach them the truth of Jesus—with a compliment connected to their misguided beliefs no less.

Outreach doesn't require you to compromise your values and it never should contradict the Word of God.

But it does require you to think differently. It requires you to consider what people who don't believe what you believe care about, worry about, and want. While it doesn't pander to their values, it considers how to build a bridge to those who are indifferent or even hostile toward our most deeply held beliefs.

Since outreach is concerned with building a bridge, the methods a church might use are as varied as the people we reach out to. Life.Church, pastored by Craig Groeschel, has adopted the maxim, "Anything short of sin."[2] While you and your church may or may not be willing to go that far, there are a number of outreach ministry opportunities and methods to choose from. Consider several of these common (as well as emerging) outreach ministries currently employed in churches around the country.

Children's Events and Programming

In 2004, George Barna released the ministry-transforming finding that 64 percent of people who give their lives to Jesus do so before they turn eighteen years old.[3] Children's events and programming may be the most important and effective outreach ministry at your church. It's not a new idea, but it has endured because it works. Children's programs and events build a bridge to kids through fun activities and high-energy learning. And the prospect of involving their kids or even the free childcare the programs offer often reaches parents.

---

2   https://open.life.church/training/44-anything-short-of-sin

3   https://www.barna.com/research/evangelism-is-most-effective-among-kids

• Clubs

In the 1950s the children's ministry known as AWANA was launched. Over the next decades, a number of evangelistic club programs followed suit. Most of them have a strong emphasis on Bible memorization, games, activities, and awards that are centered on Bible learning. A number of publishers have developed complete club programs; some churches opt to build their own. Usually, the clubs meet during a midweek evening. They provide solid Bible learning, but also require highly committed volunteers.

• VBS

Churches have been providing Vacation Bibles Schools for decades as well. The three-to-five-day programs usually provide high-energy songs, crafts, games, Bible story presentations, and snacks! There are a variety of complete VBS kits available with a tremendous difference in total cost per child. Most VBS programs include a day where kids have an opportunity to decide to follow Jesus. Many churches report a large number of children making that commitment every year. You might be surprised to find how many adults in your church became Christians at a VBS!

The Vacation Bible School model has given way to other similar three-to-five-day programs that provide a different focus. Sports camps have become common outreach programs at churches where kids hone their athletic skills while learning truths from God's Word. Some churches have launched similar programs focusing on science experiments or the arts. One emerging model is the wilderness survival camp where kids might learn how to eat bugs and build shelters while drawing near to God.

• Special Events

One effective way to bring new children to your church is through attractional events, and even entertainment. Movie nights complete with popcorn or concessions are a low-cost yet effective way to bring in new kids. Some churches have indoor drive-ins where kids create and decorate their own "cars" to sit in during the movie. Other churches take the movies to underserved neighborhoods with outdoor screens and projection systems. A simple variation of this outreach is a treasure hunt, which allows the members of your church to invite in new people to a relaxed and fun atmosphere.

For a unique, but sometimes expensive, event, your church can bring in a special act or entertainer. There are a number of Christian magicians, ventriloquists, and groups who will keynote your outreach. Outreach.com has a list of seasoned and proven acts that deliver a night of laughter and cheering at your church.[4]

• Needs-Based Outreach

A powerful and effective method to reach children is to go to them instead of bringing them to your church. Finding needs in your community—and meeting them—opens huge doors for sharing the gospel. For example, tutoring programs, backyard Bible clubs, and language classes bring God's Word to new areas and also demonstrate the love of Jesus to your whole community. There's nothing like seeing the church caring for needs of

---

4   See https://www.outreach.com/events/christian-speakers. aspx

others to help the unchurched reconsider their beliefs and thoughts on the Bride of Christ.

The Roles

The beauty of outreach to children is that it provides a place for nearly every sort of person in your church to serve. Clubs and VBS programs need enthusiastic and creative teachers and speakers, small group leaders who are willing to shepherd kids through the program, music leaders, as well as games and craft leaders. There is no end to behind-the-scenes roles as well.

Some of the roles don't even require that you really like working with kids! Children's programs need help with check-in and registration, organizing and gathering supplies, accounting, decorating, preparing snacks, and marketing. Security teams provide safety and a sense of comfort for parents who drop their kids off.

Leadership gifts are essential to any children's ministry effort. Children's events usually work best with a point person who develops a leadership team to guide the heart and purpose of the ministry, make decisions, and direct purchasing.

God will use all these ministry roles together to change the course of eternity for many children in your community! If you have a chance at your church to reach out to children—don't pass it up!

Interest and Specialty Groups

Many people in your community will never even consider coming to your church—even on Christmas and Easter. However, everyone has interests and hobbies. One great way to make a connection with them is to build a bridge through a common interest. In your interest groups outreaches, be sensitive to the timing and forcefulness with which you share the gospel. No one likes a bait and switch presentation, and the unchurched are no exception. If your genuine goal is to build a relationship, the time to share the gospel will eventually present itself as the Holy Spirit leads you.

• Men's Activities

Some churches have had tremendous success reaching men through Saturday-morning pancake breakfasts, life training, and empowerment programs such as Men's Fraternity (mensfraternity.com) or Wild at Heart events (ransomedheart.com). Men looking for help in their marriages, parenting, or businesses are especially drawn to these events. Other churches have found that younger men are drawn to less-structured activities.

Consider what the men in your community care about. If you live in an area focused on the outdoors consider starting archery, shooting, hiking, athletic leagues, kayaking, four wheeling, or fishing groups. Men typically respond well to opportunities to serve together in building, repair, or maintenance. Be ready to see how unchurched men will engage in church activities when you give them a chance to work on behalf of others.

It's not only acceptable to be a nerd—it's desirable. Leverage that fact by emphasizing your desire to geek out together in groups that focus on strategy games, photography and graphic design, and even online games. If you're willing to be edgy, consider that a number of churches have used recent interest in axe throwing to reach out to the community and even whisky tasting or homebrew clubs. Of course, these efforts are more readily embraced by members of some denominations than others.

• Women's Activities

Nearly every community offers a "Mothers of Preschoolers" MOPS (mops.org) group or some sort of hybrid equivalent program. Young mothers need support and a break. You can provide the encouraging, caring, and welcoming atmosphere they're craving. Do so, and you'll discover how unchurched women will meet at your church, find belonging, and then come to a saving belief in Jesus!

Traditional women's interest groups provide an opportunity for people in your church to invite their friends into relationship with women at your church. Craft events, gardening groups, canning, quilting, and empty-nester groups have been proven to work. However, if you want to reach new women in your community, prepare to go beyond gender stereotypes. Hiking, biking, as well as nearly every interest targeted at men provide excellent opportunities to reach women in your community as well. Here's the edgy idea for women's ministry: some churches are finding great success reaching women by taking a practice with questionable roots (such as yoga) and flipping it to focus on bringing glory to Jesus through worship and prayer.

• Youth Activities

Pizza and games have been bringing kids to Jesus for decades, and they're still surprisingly effective outreach tools. Youth activities focused on adrenaline, fun, and new experiences provide great opportunities for your teenagers to invite their friends. Creative selfie scavenger hunts and challenges to make videos and Vines appeal to many young people as well. Some youth are drawn to big high-energy events, while many are hungry for more intimate conversation and care over coffee with a few friends. Don't forget the power of outreach initiated by the youth in your church. They can build bridges and relationships with other students that your adult never could by taking friends to lunch, coffee, or other events they love.

• **Family Activities**

Church ministries and outreaches often split families up and send family members in different directions. Since so much of the responsibilities and activities families engage in already separate them, why not bring them together? Hosting a family game night or reserving a few hours at a miniature golf course can help entire families come and connect with the families of your church. Outreach is one of the few ministries in your church that your whole family can often do together!

The Roles

Anyone in your church with an interest or hobby has the ability to reach out to others simply by inviting others to learn about it. Large events, comedy nights, and expos (such as a hunting or crafts expo) provide a multitude of opportunities for various roles including marketing, fundraising, registration, decoration, setup, and leadership. You might find some potential leaders with a passion for their hobby coupled with a deathly fear of leading and organizing others. Pair them with people who aren't afraid to minister and speak to others, allowing the hobby expert to shine when knowledge about the hobby is needed. The more outgoing partner can include a quick faith lesson at each gathering.

Potentially hazardous activities such as archery or axe throwing need to have assistants who are knowledgeable and focused exclusively on safety guidelines. Nearly every effort discussed in this section rises and falls on the willingness of your church members to invite others who share an interest in these events. Help them understand they play the most important role on the outreach team.

Going Beyond the Church Walls

Most of the strategies mentioned in this chapter, while often effective, are also relatively comfortable because they either take place within the church or rely on people in the church to establish a critical mass for a successful group or event. Churches reaching their community know they must go beyond the walls and people of their own congregation. Rather than expecting people to come to church, they go where the people are. If you want to reach people no one else is reaching, you have to do things no one else is doing!

• Community Partnering

It's important to serve the needs of your community simply because God's Word directs us to do so. James 1:27 reminds us that religion God accepts as pure looks after widows and orphans in their distress. A few wonderful outcomes of obedience to this command are the bridges it builds to those you serve, the doors it opens to presenting the gospel, and the favor it brings to the church from those in your community who aren't served but witness your good deeds.

The simplest way to meet community needs is to partner with existing organizations in your community who are already meeting needs. Pregnancy centers, food distribution centers, and shelters provide an amazing opportunity for you to reach out while finding your niche and passion. Many followers of Jesus reach kids in their community by coaching at local rec centers and having their church sponsor the team. Your church may not always get the recognition, but if you partner with a Christian organization, Jesus still will!

• Meeting a Different Need

You don't have to look too hard to find needs that aren't currently being met by other organizations in your community. If God has given you a burden or even a mild concern for such needs, it's likely he's asking you to do something about it. There is no end to the variety of need-based outreaches you can launch. Many churches find creative solutions to help with school supplies, car maintenance for single moms or widows, diaper and formula drives, deliveries for shut-ins, home repair, and yard maintenance for the disabled or elderly. Some churches have taken these sorts of ministries to the streets by outfitting trailers or buses as mobile food and poverty relief services. You can reach out in a powerful way by visiting and praying for the sick at your hospital or starting a Bible study at your local jail.

• (Not so Random) Acts of Kindness

Kindness builds bridges. Romans 2:4 reminds us that God's kindness leads to repentance. Kindness in itself is a form of outreach as it lifts spirits and demonstrates how God values people. However, being intentional to connect the acts of kindness to your church or Jesus also builds bridges by helping people reconsider their negative beliefs or opinions about the church. It also forces people who don't really think about faith or church to consider it for a moment in a positive way. The easiest way to make the connection is simply to attach a card identifying your church with the act. For example, if you pass out flowers, make sure each one has a card with your church information attached to it.

Churches often empower their members to pay for the coffee of the next customer in line, feeding parking meters, handing out water bottles on trails, and carrying out groceries. You can bring these acts to the next level by installing playground equipment, maintaining trails, or building a community garden. Any act of kindness you can think of can be done in Jesus' name!

The Roles

All of our outreach ideas and efforts should be covered in serious prayer, as it invites God's awesome power and transformation into our small efforts. However, when you go out into the community, special care should be given to develop prayer teams to ask for God's protection, direction, and efficacy. These sorts of outreach efforts usually also need one or two people on each team who are bold and have the gift of faith or evangelism. Almost all of these efforts feel awkward and intimidating at first, but once someone breaks the ice, they become joyful and fun!

Most of these efforts need people who like to organize, people who like to connect with others, and people who like to work. Your outreach effort will be much more effective if you include all of these gifts on your team! As you partner with other organization or your community, look for people with community connections who will ask for permission, funding, or assistance.

CHAPTER 6

FINDING YOUR BEST FIT

Just Start

*D*o you want to find your call? Are you hungry to make a difference for the kingdom of God? Do you feel there is more to life? There is a guaranteed way to find what you're looking for: *start*. God can't steer a parked a car. But once you get going, you'll be amazed at the places God will take you, the doors he will open for you, and things he teaches you.

Pastor Ken is the senior leader of a network of churches that reaches well over 1,800 people every week in southwestern Colorado. His ministry journey began nearly two decades ago, but not with seminary, Bible college, or even teaching a class. He first served by answering his children's pastor's call for help with preschool. His first job was to work a puppet from behind a table for a half-dozen preschoolers who were squirming on the floor.

Ken recounts the sheer terror he felt that Sunday morning. "I don't know how six preschool children had such power. But I was terrified as I held the puppet above the table. My voice cracked as I spoke. I literally had to wipe the sweat off my forehead as I read the script word for word, sometimes forgetting to move the puppets' mouth."

Despite the ordeal, Ken kept serving in children's ministry for the next couple of years, filling various roles.

The children's pastor who had recruited him eventually took a position as the youth minister of the church. To his surprise, the senior pastor approached Ken and asked him if he'd serve as the unpaid children's pastor. Not knowing at the time that there is no end to unpaid pastoral and leadership roles in churches, Ken was honored that he was being considered.

For three years he served in that slot, and then he was offered a position as the small groups pastor at the same church. Soon the senior pastor brought Ken a new opportunity—to serve as a church planting pastor in a nearby community. That experience opened up the door for Ken to become executive pastor in the church where he currently serves as the senior leader.

When he signed up to be a preschool puppeteer, Ken had no idea where that decision would lead him. Deep down, he felt a nudge—not really a call—to pastoral ministry. But one yes led to another opportunity. Another yes led to another opportunity, and God brought Ken to a place where he currently feels he's in his sweet spot. He sees hundreds of people give their lives to Jesus every year.

If you want to find your sweet spot in outreach ministry, you have to begin reaching out! Some Christians never start because the opportunities God brings them don't quite fit their big dream and call. You don't have to spend too much time in church before you'll run across someone with a dream to reach a group with a pressing need. Let's say they'd like to start a ranch to reach out to troubled youth. The question for them is, "What are you doing for troubled youth now right where God has you?" Too many people would have to answer, "Not much." Sometimes the big vision for the future gets in the way of the little difference God wants to make through them right now. But why would God give them a ranch in the mountains for ministry if they won't minister in their own neighborhood?

God isn't looking for dreams and visions as much as he's looking for faithfulness. As we are faithful with little opportunities, God prepares us and trains us for bigger possibilities. The very best way to find your fit is literally to start something—nearly anything!

Jesus tells us to store up treasure in Heaven while we live on this earth. One of the greatest treasures you could find in Heaven is to look around when you get there and see someone who is there because you led them to Jesus. So many followers of Jesus don't ever have the opportunity to lead someone to Christ simply because they never start any sort of outreach. Often fear or the pressures of busyness hold them back. What amazing opportunities are to be found if they'd only begin.

For example, simply by starting you may find that prison ministry isn't a good fit for you, or that leading an interest group is more pain than work. But at the very least, you'll find an outreach strategy you can cross off your list. More likely, you'll gain valuable tools, insight, and experiences for the next outreach effort where God calls you.

Then What?

After you begin, you can do a number of things to find your outreach ministry fit. First, take note of the activities you enjoy—and the ones you dread. So many ministry skills are transferable. If you're good at organizing a onetime outreach for your small group, it's likely you'll be effective at organizing a large outreach or event. No one is good at everything. If it's not a good fit, you'll likely serve the kingdom of God better if you avoid that specific type of work in the future.

God isn't honored by self-inflicted misery, and no one has ever grumbled or complained someone else into a relationship with Jesus. But be careful of throwing out the whole idea just because your approach or role was a bad fit. Sometimes, trying again with some minor tweaks can make all the difference. The wrong timing, the wrong message, or even the wrong audience can sink an otherwise wonderful idea. Certainly you've tasted a food you thought you didn't like until it was served correctly; or an activity you hated until you made a change in your grip, method, or attitude. Outreach can work like that.

In every outreach effort you undertake, watch for fruitfulness. If you find that people engage and respond when you speak, you should look for (or create) more chances to speak. If you can tell that your behind-the-scenes service is making a big difference, then do more of it! Ultimately, fruit is God's responsibility. Your responsibility is faithfulness. But God wants your life to bear fruit, and watching for it can help you find the best ways to produce it in the future.

Accelerate the Process

Even though nothing's better than getting started, several tools and approaches can help you find your fit a little faster. First, get to know yourself a little better. Take any one of several personality assessments to discover more about who you are. Each one has a slightly different nuance. The DISC (discpersonalitytesting.com), Myers Briggs (myersbriggs.org), and CliftonStrengths (gallup. com/cliftonstrengths) assessments are commonly used in churches and workplaces to help people understand themselves. As you complete each assessment, pay special attention to what they say about the approach you should take to outreach. For example, the DISC test can help you understand how you respond to challenges and how you influence others. Such knowledge can have a profound impact on what outreach activity you choose and how you do it.

First Corinthians 12:4, 5 says, "There are different kinds of gifts, but the same Spirit distributes them. There are different kinds of service, but the same Lord." Spiritual gifts are connected with your personality, skills, and preferences, but that's not all. They are unique gifts and abilities given to you by God's Spirit for the purpose of advancing the kingdom of God.

Familiarize yourself with the various spiritual gifts listed in the Bible. Start by reading 1 Corinthians 12–14, Romans 12:3-13, and Ephesians 4:1-16. Pay attention to the gifts listed in Scripture and consider which ones seem to fit you.

A variety of printed and online inventories can help you discern your spiritual gifts. One of the most complete assessments is a small book titled, *Discover Your Spiritual Gifts the Network Way* by Bruce L. Bugbee. It includes four assessments, including one you send out to three friends to get their insights and feedback on your gifts.

As you begin to understand your gifts, apply them to your outreach methods. For example, if you have the spiritual gift of hospitality, volunteer for roles focused on making people feel welcomed and included in your outreach efforts. You'll think of small touches that make a big difference that other leaders with different gifts would never even consider.

The fact that you are reading this book shows you are already on the fast track to your outreach sweet spot! Keep sharpening your outreach gifts, tools, and approaches. There are so many opportunities for live-streamed and in-person ministry conferences. Nearly all of them provide some training and inspiration on outreach, as well as opportunities to network with others who are finding ways to reach the unchurched in their communities. There are also a number of publishers, podcasts, books, and training sites that focus on outreach methods and ideas. We've included in this book (Chapters 13 and 14) a number of helpful outreach organizations and resources, as you continue in the mission of leading others to Jesus!

You don't need a seminary degree to share the gospel with others. In fact, if you have found salvation in Jesus, you have extensive firsthand knowledge of what others need! 1 Peter 3:15 challenges us, "Always be prepared to give an answer to everyone who asks you to give the reason for the hope that you have." If you are going to reach out to people who don't know Jesus, you should be prepared to lead them to him. Even if you fill a behind-the-scenes role in outreach efforts, God will likely bring you an opportunity to share your faith with someone who needs hope.

Are you ready? It won't take long to get there! First, just think about your own story. It is the most powerful tool you have for sharing the gospel with others. Some people like to have a longer, five-to ten-minute version to share over coffee and a one-minute version to share at a booth or event. Don't worry about coming up with a script or canned comments; just think through the major details and trust that Holy Spirit will guide you. Consider also being ready to lead someone through the major truths of the gospel to the place where they will make a personal commitment to Jesus.

The famous "Roman Road" can give you the most important truths of the gospel. As you start reaching out to others, consider working on committing these verses to memory: Romans 3:23; 6:23; 5:8; 10:9, 6:4, and 8:1. Remember not to force conversations with people, but look for opportunities to lead them to Christ. Be bold! If you want to lead someone to Jesus, you'll need to start asking people if they want to come to know him.

After "Just start," the most important aspect of finding your ministry fit is simply, "Don't stop." Remember that outreach is a spiritual work that is bringing the power, salvation, and freedom of God into places of spiritual darkness. If you never experience resistance or difficulty in your walk with God, perhaps part of the reason is that you aren't much of a threat to the Enemy. As you reach out, you can expect rejection, disappointment, anxiety, and conflict. Of course, you should work to overcome these obstacles with solid communication, constant prayer, good planning, and sensitive outreach approaches. After all, when Peter challenges us to be prepared to share our faith, he also immediately says to do so "with gentleness and respect." But don't be surprised if you encounter times when the effort just didn't feel right or goes wrong. When—not *if*—it does, make adjustments, change your role, or adjust your strategy. But don't stop. God promises in

Galatians 6:9 that you will reap a harvest at the proper time if you don't give up!

The Great Commission was given to all of us, not just those with special talents or certain personalities. There is certainly a place for a person with your gifts and talents within Jesus' command to make disciples. What's more, the church needs you to find your fit. There are people only you can reach! There are so many roles, ways, and places where you can reach out. What's more, there are many people who are far from God right now, people who are waiting desperately for you to reach out to them!

SECTION 3

OUTREACH IDEAS, TIPS, AND TOOLS

CHAPTER 7

121 OUTREACH IDEAS

6 Community Outreach Events

1. Sponsor a **jewelry-making booth** for kids at your community's next big event or farmer's market. In your booth, set up bracelet-making stations at a table. At each station provide various beads on sectioned plates and tape one end of a length of string to the plate (or tie a knot on one end). Make sure volunteers are ready to set up new stations and help kids tie their completed bracelets on their wrists.

   Consider providing a simple, written explanation of the gospel that uses different-colored beads as visual aids. Green beads represent God's creation. Gray represents sin. Red is for God's amazing love and sacrifice. Blue stands for faith. Yellow represents Heaven. Remember that beads can be a choking hazard for little ones, so provide another option like finger painting for children under five-years-old.

2. With your church, **rent an entire bowling alley** and invite the community to spend the evening bowling for free! Or if your budget won't allow renting the whole facility, choose just some of the lanes. (In this case, provide clear signs to direct guests to your free lanes.)

3. Ask permission from the manager or owner of your local **drive-in movie theater** to **wash the windshields** of cars waiting in line before they're allowed to enter. While paper towels and window cleaner will work, squeegees and buckets will get it done faster. Do not except donations from drivers, but give cards that say, "Compliments of Name of Your Church" and thank them for the opportunity to serve.

4. Hold an **expo for a hobby or activity** popular in your community. For example, if your community is known for hiking, invite local sports equipment stores to set up displays during your expo. Find local experts who can give workshops or demonstrations on skills like orienteering or wilderness survival. Include raffles, giveaways, and church information for everyone who comes. Make sure to include local experts who also attend your congregation.

5. Sponsor a **kite festival** for your community on your church grounds or a local park. Make certain there are no power lines, large trees, or other hazards in your flying areas. Give each arriving family a free kite with string and information about your church. Throughout the day you can hold events such as kite making, decorating, combat kite wars, aerial acrobatics competition, and foil and cellular kite demonstrations.

6. Challenge every family in your church **to invite their neighbors for a barbecue** at their homes. Give each participating family a barbecue kit that includes customizable door-hanger invites, a prayer guide for

their neighborhood, a few recipes, a checklist for getting ready for the barbecue, and some safety tips for inviting others into their homes. Delivering the kit in an oven mitt with your church logo will generate extra excitement for the effort. For the greatest impact, time the barbecue challenge to coincide with a sermon series on loving and reaching out to your neighbors.

7 Seasonal Outreaches

1. **Give away cocoa at school bus stops** in chilly weather. Label each cup with your church name. About thirty minutes before the peak commute time, set up a table near a bus stop with a large, insulated carafe or thermos full of hot chocolate. As people wait at or approach the stop, offer them a free cup of cocoa.

2. Create small **May Day baskets** to deliver to a neighborhood. Include candy, flowers, lip balm, a simple craft, and an invite (or information) about your church. Deliver these door-to-door; ring the doorbell and then leave without waiting for someone to answer.

3. **Give Mother's Day flowers.** At least three weeks ahead of time, contact your local grocery store or flower shop to order flowers. Look for deals on bulk orders of carnations or roses and make certain the flowers will be available two days before Mother's Day. Create business cards that say, "Happy Mother's Day!" on one side and, "Your friends at The Name of Your Church" on the other. Punch a hole in each card and fasten one to each flower stem using a twisty tie or a rubber band. You can simply find a crowded sidewalk to pass them out or get permission to conduct this outreach at a grocery store or business. Give a flower to every woman you see. If a person protests, "I'm not a mother," simply say, "We think you deserve a flower anyway."

4. **Give frozen fruit treats to families as they leave sports fields in warm weather.** Stock a cooler with ice and treats. (Fla-Vor-Ice freezer bars or Otter Pops ice

pops come in their own sleeves and won't make a mess when they start melting.) Station your group between the fields and the parked cars to avoid disrupting the games and practices. Set up a table with a sign that says, "Stay cool with a free treat from Your Church Name. Way to go out there!"

5. **Deliver Thanksgiving meals** to under-resourced families. Create turkey boxes that each include a frozen turkey, canned goods, and vegetables that keep (*e.g.,* potatoes and onions). Include an invite or brochure from your church. Distribute to families you know, get recommendations from local agencies, or simply ask people in your church for nominations.

6. **Distribute glow sticks at your community Christmas festival, tree-lighting ceremony, parade, or winter carnival.** Imprint these with your church logo and information or attach a card with a ribbon to each stick. Consider using this approach to advertise your church's special Christmas services.

7. Hold a **Christmas festival.** Station a table with roasted chestnuts and hot cocoa outside the entrance. Include a path with Christmas light displays, a live nativity, or rides on a horse-drawn trailer. On the inside of your building include carolers, cookie-decorating stations, and winter-themed games.

8 Ways to Reach Out with Random Acts of Kindness

1. **Prepare free popcorn kits for movie renters.** Print double-sided business cards that say, "A gift for you" on one side and the name or logo of your church on the back. Tape the card on a packet of microwave popcorn with "A gift for you" facing out. Put the tape on the top of the card so people will easily be able to flip it up to see your church information. Put a strip of double-sided tape on the back of the popcorn packet and stick it to a DVD kiosk. Recruit a team to prepare a quantity of the packets. Then give them to church members who will stick a popcorn packet to a kiosk every time they go by one.

2. **Give away hand sanitizer.** Work with an imprint company to create customized one-half ounce bottles. Print "A gift for you" at the top of the bottle with your church logo underneath it. Distribute these to church members who will place the bottles on gas pumps every time they fill up.

3. **Reach out to those visiting self-serve laundries.** Call this outreach "Loads of Love." Get permission from a laundry to set up a table with individual bags of snacks, free detergent, rolls of quarters, and information about the church. Do this once a week or more, depending on your capacity. Set up the table and staff it with volunteers who will interact with patrons and be available for prayer or a listening ear if it is requested. Include information about your church, Scripture portions, or a list of community resources for recreation, family help, or financial aid.

4. **Set up a little library in an underserved neighborhood** in your area. Purchase the little wooden library houses or have someone at your church make them. Get permission from property owners to place the box. Include a sign that says, "Take a book, return it when you're done" instead of the usual "Take a book, leave a book." Regularly stock the library with books that have a strong positive or faith message. For additional information about little libraries, visit littlefreelibrary. org.

5. **Bring water or pizza to share with kids at your local skate park.** Ask your youth pastor for advice on the best strategy and safety guidelines. For example, always do this in pairs of two adults.

6. **Partner with your community's adopt-a-road program.** You will commit to remove the trash on your assigned road. The program often includes a sign on that road naming your church as the adopter. You will likely agree to a certain number of clean-ups per year and to follow the city's procedures and training.

7. Ask permission from a grocery store to **help people carry their groceries** and load them into their cars. To reduce suspicion, set up a table near the door with a sign that includes the name of your church and a message like "The Kindness Project" or "Make a Difference Day." As people bring their carts to the door, ask them if you can help them to the car. Make it clear that you won't accept tips.

8. Recruit a team of those who like to knit to **create sets of baby-sized booties and beanies.** Include a tag on each that says, "Handknit with love at Name of Your Church." Deliver them to a local hospital as a gift for every newborn who arrives there.

10 Ways to Reach Out in a Crisis

1. **Seek balance.** Don't minimize, over spiritualize, or overplay what is happening. Try to gather facts and offer concrete actions that you can legitimately do. Observe guidelines and instructions issued by authorities. Is it collecting food or supplies? Is it offering prayers? Is it giving what you have to a neighbor? Remember the Stockdale Paradox: never waiver in your faith or turn this crisis into the defining moment in your life, but always confront the brutal facts of the crisis.

2. **Listen** to those in need. This could be neighbors, friends, relatives, or strangers. Be prepared with encouragement, but not platitudes. Believe in them and pray with them.

3. **Acknowledge the grief** that many are feeling. Understand that all affected will go through the grieving process, all at different times, sometimes getting stuck, sometimes going backward, sometimes skipping a stage. Learn about the stages: denial, anger, bargaining, depression, and acceptance. (Some models include other stages.) Be ready to listen to those affected and ask questions, helping them see where they are in their grief. Do not judge. Allow them to grieve in whatever stage they're in. Join in their grieving if it's appropriate. Offer grace and understanding. Don't offer platitudes. Offer prayers if they're open to it. Don't fill silence unless the Holy Spirit strongly prompts. Check in regularly and ask questions to help your friend/acquaintance determine where they are and what they can do to move forward without pressuring or adding guilt.

4. **Contact local authorities** to find out what you can do to help, and then do one of the items on their list. Only commit to something you can do without adding more responsibility to the local authorities.

5. Write **notes of encouragement and prayer to the first responders**. Determine the best way to deliver them to someone who can distribute them.

6. Consider the **behind-the-scenes helpers** and **reach out to them** with encouragement, prayers, or other appropriate help. Who is cleaning the restrooms, collecting the garbage, answering the phones, responding to e-mails, running the homeless shelters? Consider how you can minister to them.

7. Recruit a team to **pray for neighborhoods.** Make notes that say, "Name of Your Church prayed for you and your neighborhood today." Send people from your church to walk throughout their neighborhoods to pray. Have them use blue or red colored ribbons to tie the note to a stop sign or street sign in the neighborhood.

8. Create a **simple sheet with the header "How Can I Help?"** On the remainder of the page, include services your church members might provide for their neighbors in crisis. Possibilities: "Pick up Groceries," "Provide Transportation to the Doctor," "Stop by to Talk," "Just Pray for Me." Provide a place where your church members can include their names and contact information. Encourage them to **post the**

flyers at their neighbors' doors and follow up when contacted.

9. Start a new **social media kindness page or group** to connect people in need during the crisis. Give it a simple name like "The Name of Your Community Cares." Include guidelines for posts such as no bullying or swearing. Explain that the page has been created for community members to meet each other's needs. Start a number of threads such as "Food Needed," "Diapers Needed," or "County Updates." Recruit one or two people from your church to moderate it and move the new posts to the correct thread. Start by inviting church members.

10. **Share stories** with those you're serving about how your family has met hard times well. When appropriate, share how God was a part of those times. Talk about how your family (or whoever you're talking with) can look forward and make this a time that's remembered in positive terms. Give God the credit as often as is appropriate.

6 Ways to Reach Out to Local Businesses

1. **Arrange power lunches.** Find a member of your church who works in the center of your community's business district. Ask him or her to find a conference room or dining area to host a thirty-minute Bible study once per week over the lunch hour. Encourage a few members of your church to attend and to bring one business associate along every week. Cover topics that career-minded people are concerned with such as the Biblical approach to conflict, setting priorities, and forgiving others. For extra impact, provide lunch for everyone who comes.

2. **Join networking groups and associations.** Possibilities: the local chamber of commerce, the Small Business Administration, or Rotary International. Learn the names of those who attend. Eventually consider volunteering or leading a committee to build relationships with others.

3. **Clean bathrooms or windows** at small businesses. Grab some cleaning supplies and go from business to business asking where you could clean. Assure the employees that you won't accept money or anything in return. As employees ask you why you want to clean their bathrooms, explain that you just want to show God's love to them and that your church wants to show appreciation for the contribution their business makes to your community.

4. **Sponsor a local networking breakfast** that brings business leaders together and shows your church's

support of businesses in the area. Find a respected leader in your church or community to keynote the breakfast and then host the event at your church. Advertise the event through direct mail and social media. Recruit business owners in your church to attend and to invite business leaders they know. Focus on building relationships and providing value to local businesses.

5. **Create a directory or a web page on your church website that lists locally owned businesses in your area.**

6. Reach out to **local business owners** who **can teach a class or seminar** on something the people in your church want to learn about. Possibilities: investing, tax advice, bicycle repair, or marriage and family therapy. Host the seminars at your church building or at the speaker's place of business. Make sure you mention their business before they begin. Consider pairing the nonchurch members with members of your church who are in the same field to teach the class together.

5 Ways to Serve First Responders

1. **Offer your parking lot, building, and campus as a free space for regular training required by law enforcement agencies in your area.** Make certain everyone is out of their way during the training session. Explain that your only requirement is that your team will be allowed to serve lunch as a way to say thank-you for the service they provide and risks they take.

2. **Recruit kids to create thank-you cards for first responders.** Ask your children's pastor to set aside time every week for a few weeks to create the cards. Have them focus on a different group every week such as law enforcement, fire fighters, paramedics, and emergency room staff. Encourage kids to include drawings of the responders in action. For even more impact, have some of the kids join you in delivering the cards along with some baked goodies.

3. **Prepare gender-specific landing packs for the difficult times when law enforcement officers have to remove children from their home** or arrest their guardians. These children are often placed in emergency foster care with little to no supplies. Include emergency items like toothbrushes, a pillow, blankets, two or three days of clothing, and a comfort item like a stuffed animal. Contact your local law enforcement office to see if they'd like to keep the packs on hand or if they'd like you to deliver them within 24 hours of the placement. Pack the items in a quality duffle bag. As far as you are able, make certain kids know that the packs and all the contents belong to them wherever they go.

4. **Give gift cards from a local coffee shop.** Ask for a list of first names of employees at a local fire station or police precinct. Purchase a gift card for each person, one that will cover the cost of at least one specialty coffee. (Explain what you're doing, and the coffee shop may give you a discount!) Write thank-you notes to each person including an encouraging Scripture verse. Some possible verses include Deuteronomy 31:6, Isaiah 40:31, Isaiah 41:10, and 2 Corinthians 12:9. Sign the card, "Your friends at Name of Your Church."

5. **Plan a "Day of Honor" Sunday at your church** and invite first responders from throughout your area to attend. To prepare, collect stories on the work of first responders in your area through the newspaper, county and city social media pages, interviews, and word of mouth. Create a number of awards to give various first responders for their efforts over the last year. Possibilities: "Uncommon Valor," "An Uncommon Difference," "Uncommon Concern and Care." Purchase quality medals for each award. Notify the departments of the officers receiving the awards and tell the local press, too.

   At the weekend service, invite the officers to come forward to receive the awards. Ask your pastor to give a short talk on uncommon honor when you present the awards.

12 Ways to Serve the Oppressed and Under Resourced

1. **Adopt a local low-income apartment complex.** With the permission of the manager, get to know the families. Offer activities to encourage those families (homework help, financial advice, job counseling, food, etc.). The key is building relationships. Develop a team of people from your church that will visit weekly. Offer to pray for each family you know and follow-up to see how the prayers were answered. Let God lead each step.

2. **Compile a list of community resources** that help those in need: food banks, clothing banks, other ministries, government programs, school programs, rental assistance, help with paying utilities, school programs, Head Start, counseling, businesses that make donations, etc. Make sure your list is available in whatever languages are common in your area. Offer your list to all of the organizations on your list as well as any families you become aware of. Post your list electronically so others can easily share it.

3. **Talk with the administration of a school that has low-income families. Ask how you can most help the school** meet the needs of those families. Come up with a plan for the resources, people, time, and facilities. Return to the administration with your plan and ask for their permission and blessing. Be sure you detail how you will be sharing your faith. Be sure you can carry out the plan as outlined before you begin.

4. **Partner with a ministry** that is successfully meeting the needs of those who are homeless, unemployed,

or under resourced. Decide how you can help meet needs. You may start alone and then include others from your church or other churches in your community. Love INC is one national resource (loveinc.org) to help you get started.

5. **Provide a job center** where you help people get training and find jobs available in your area. There are many online resources that will help provide training and certificates in employable areas. Many churches are doing this well. One example is Manna Connect at Cherry Hills Community Church in Highlands Ranch, Colorado (mannaconnect.org).

6. Start and help maintain a **community garden** in a low-income area. Recruit fellow gardener friends. Get to know those who come by. Talk with them about your gardening interests and encourage them to participate in the growing, weeding, and eating of healthy foods. Use your garden as a way to talk about how God has grown good things in your life.

7. Host a **spa night** for low-income women. Find beauticians who will come cut and style their hair. Offer manicures. Bring new makeup to give as gifts. Offer tea and fun treats. End the time by talking about the inner beauty God plants in each of them.

8. Find people who can help **provide auto repair** services. Offer a monthly time and place for people with low incomes to bring their cars for maintenance. (You may decide to start by doing this just one time).

Raise funds for the needed supplies (oil, brake fluid, and parts as needed). Partner with organizations who receive donated cars to find ways to provide cars for low-income families. Consider policies such as how many cars can one family have repaired or replaced, how much of the expense should they pay (0, $10, or 10 percent). Keep a database of families you help, their contact information, what help was given, and when. Hand a note to each recipient about why you're doing this, including a prayer for them.

9. Join a local **prison ministry**. Go through the training and become a regular (monthly or weekly) helper. Let the Holy Spirit guide you in your conversations.

10. **Create gift kits for those who are homeless.** Put these items together in plastic sacks: sanitizing wipes, a bottle of water, nutritious snacks, lip balm, sunscreen, a devotional, and information about your church. Give these instead of money to those on the street seeking help. Distribute the kits to church members who will keep them in their cars to hand out instead of money. Make sure everyone taking the kits also receives instruction about safety protocols and procedures for approaching and interacting with those who are homeless.

11. **Get to know a person who is homeless.** Look around and ask God to direct you. Talk with them and ask them about their life. Refrain from giving them money. Figure out together what would be most helpful to them. Share your faith honestly and ask them questions about theirs.

12. **Offer ESL (English as a Second Language) classes.**
There are many options available for this—everything from purchased curriculum to just offering to meet and talk with those who want to practice their English. Choose what's right for you and those who want to help you. Include your faith in your conversation as naturally as talking about the weather.

6 Ways to Connect or Follow-up with Visitors

1. **Connect each visitor with a tour guide.** Make the tour guides easily identifiable with lanyards or shirts. Tour guides can help with the check-in process for children's ministry, help get coffee, and share about programs and connection points at the church. Train every ministry and member at your church to allow tour guides and visitors to cut to the front of any line others might need to wait in.

2. **Offer a first-timers reception** after every service, or at least once a month. Invite all newcomers to come to a designated area immediately after the service to meet the pastor and other church leaders. Provide refreshments and informational materials about your church. Have the pastor welcome the group, share an idea on how to connect at the church, and welcome questions.

3. **Recruit a number of volunteers willing to build bridges and relationships with visitors.** You might call them "What's Next Leaders." If you have a visitor's card or registration process, include an option where visitors can choose, "I'd like to get a coffee or lunch with a leader from the church." Have your What's Next Leaders follow up with the visitors by taking them out. Encourage your leaders to develop a shepherding mindset for the visitors they've adopted by praying for them, continuing to reach out to them, and caring for them even if the visitors don't come back.

4. **Set up a text messaging service** to reach and communicate with people at your church. During

weekend worship, ask visitors to take out their phones and join the service. Set up the service to send an instant text message to welcome them to your church. Every week or two send a follow-up text inviting visitors to relevant events at your church. Make sure it's easy for them to opt out of the service as well.

5. **Develop a short "How Did We Do?" survey and give it to every visitor.** Include a few questions that will help you understand the visitor experience at your church. Make sure you provide a place where you ask visitors if you can follow up with them to learn more. Following up will not only help you improve; it will also help you to start building relationships with your visitors.

6. **Conduct follow-up visits with first-time guests**. Assuming you have a way to get visitors' names, recruit volunteers to call them the week after they first attend and ask if someone can drop by a welcome gift. Possibilities: a small food basket, passes to the local rec center, or gift cards to local coffee shops. Train volunteers to deliver the gift in person and to keep conversation pleasant and brief. They should deliver the gift at the door without asking to come into the home. Avoid the temptation to force deep spiritual conversations or to impose on the visitor's time and schedule.

10 Ways to Reach Families

1. **Host a family movie night**. Make sure it's an appropriate movie. Pick a theme that goes with the movie and do simple decorations. Provide a themed snack or popcorn and lemonade, or ask everyone to bring a nut-free snack to share. Encourage everyone to wear their pjs. Offer discussion questions for families for the drive home: "What was your favorite part?" "Which of the characters would you want to be?" Have someone from the church give a brief welcome and a blessing at the end.

2. **Offer parenting or marriage classes** at your church or local rec center. Here are some Christian resources to get you started: *Grace Based Parenting* by Tim Kimmel; *I May Frustrate You, but I'm A Keeper* by Ray Lincoln; *Sacred Parenting* by Gary Thomas; *Spiritual Parenting* by Michelle Anthony; *Sacred Marriage* by Gary Thomas; *The 5 Love Languages* by Gary Chapman; *The Meaning of Marriage* by Tim Keller. Make sure you have a good leader for the classes and provide small group leaders to facilitate roundtable discussions and follow-up during the week.

3. **Sponsor a family-friendly concert** at your church or local venue. Help cover the cost of the entertainment to keep admission reasonable. It could be anything from a group that tours nationally to some local bands that rotate (provided it's music you've vetted) or the worship team from your church. Be creative in making it fun and meaningful: snacks, confetti guns, balloons, and photo ops. If it's not an outwardly Christian band, have a leader of the church open and close the event appropriately.

4. **Participate in a local event/parade/fair.** Build a float for the parade, host a tent at the fair, host a table at a local event. Free bottled water is always useful. Candy is always a hit. Fun games with prizes attract families. Put stickers with a simple Christian encouragement on everything you hand out. Watch for opportunities to have spiritual conversations.

5. **Canvass the neighborhood around your church to determine their needs.** Tackle one of the biggest needs in a concrete, helpful way. Avoid the temptation to solve too many issues. Stick to one need and see it through. Be sure to inform all the families you canvassed about what you learned and what you plan to do. Go to census.gov to find a wide variety of community data to help you choose an area close to your church with criteria similar to your church's—or one that's quite different if that's your desire.

6. **Give families opportunities to serve their neighborhoods.** Parks, walking trails, and school grounds need regular cleanup. Local food and clothing banks need help sorting and organizing. Neighbors love receiving handmade cards and/or baked items. Set aside a two-hour window once a month for families to serve (all at the same time or as it works for each individual family). Encourage families to take a picture of themselves serving, then post on a bulletin board or web page. Be sure you and some of the staff families are willing to participate. Plan a celebration for all of the families who served to come together and share stories.

7. **Create welcome baskets** for families who move into the neighborhood near the church. Include information about local restaurants, churches, parks, shopping areas, and your church, along with a map. Include something to make them feel at home such as baked goods or fresh fruits and vegetables from local stores as well as a blessing card for their new home. Contact local restaurants and businesses and ask them for donations or business cards.

    If families from your church live in the neighborhood, add their location to the map with information about them on the back: "Tom and Kathy have two elementary kids and they'd love to have you over for dinner. George and Stella are retired, and they'd love to give you a tour of the neighborhood along with some insider information." When you deliver the basket, ask permission for the people noted on the map to contact them.

    A local realtor should be able to help you know when houses sell in your neighborhood. If there's a new housing area near your church, work with the builder to provide a basket for all new families there.

8. **Offer family exercise classes** at the church or sponsor them at the local rec center. Be sure you hire competent and compassionate trainers. Talk about the importance of healthy minds, bodies, and souls. Provide information about local walking trails and other ways to keep their families fit and healthy. Encourage the families to address soul health as well.

9. **Host events that help parents meet others with kids the same age.** Start with families who attend your church. Make it something engaging so they will invite others from their school or neighborhood.

    Here are a few ideas to get you started:

    *   Second-grade pool party for all the second graders and their families at a local pool or large backyard of someone in the neighborhood.

    *   "How to Survive my Child's First year in Middle School (or High School)" with several options in different rooms at the church in early June. Possibilities: a school counselor to talk about how to help your child navigate, a child psychologist who addresses the biggest fears of adolescents and how to help kids through them, a meet and greet with the principal or other administrator, a get-acquainted activity so parents meet each other and find out they have neighbors.

    *   Summer picnic for kids in the neighborhood who are entering kindergarten.

    Whatever the event, be sure the church is represented and that spiritual conversations are incorporated appropriately.

10. **Get to know a family in your neighborhood.** Invite them to your home. Don't be perfect; just be real. Find things you have in common. Ask them for things you need and offer things you have that could be helpful to them. Talk about God as naturally as you talk

about the weather without forcing an agenda. Look for opportunities to ask them about their beliefs. Engage in conversations about spiritual things, being ready to answer their questions. Invite them to activities at your church whenever it's appropriate.

7 Ways to Reach Out to Single Parents

1. **Conduct a spa day by turning a room of your church into a single-parent spa.** Ask beauticians and barbers from your church to offer free haircuts. Invite massage therapists to offer free massages and cosmetologists to offer free facials and makeup application. Make certain to provide childcare and to decorate the room and entryway to be welcoming and soothing.

2. **Host a skill day for single parents and their children.** Identify experts in your church who have skills they can share with others. Possibilities: fly fishing, sewing, guitar, kayaking, trap shooting, or archery. Set up a day for single parents in your community to bring their children to learn that skill from your experts. Make sure the event is safe. Supply all the equipment needed for the event. Other church members, your community center, and local specialty shops may lend or donate the needed equipment.

3. **Deep-clean a single parent's house.** You'll make their month! Bring supplies to clean the oven, stove, toilets, bathtubs, showers, and floors. Consider bringing a large crew into one or two homes to make a massive difference rather than small groups serving multiple homes. Have one or two workers ready to reach out and make conversation with the single parent, looking for opportunities to encourage and pray with him or her.

4. **Provide free childcare to give single parents a morning or evening break.** Purchase ads from the newspaper, radio, or social media to let single parents

know your church cares for them and wants them to have a little time to relax or catch up. Your children's ministry will be able to help you with safety procedures such as background checks for volunteers and adult-to-child ratios. Make certain you have a welcoming and complete process to check in kids including gathering parent contact information, allergy information, and any other special considerations. A few weeks after the event, send a note to each family inviting the child to join you again in your children's ministry.

5. **Stage a single mother's oil-change day at your church.** Weeks before the event, have single mothers sign up for their slot. Make sure to capture contact information and the model and year of their car so you can purchase the appropriate oil and filters in advance. Have a mechanic from your church serve as a troubleshooter for each oil-changing crew, making safety the priority. Ask each mother to sign a release of liability for the car and provide clear boundaries for your crews on the maintenance you'll provide.

6. **Help with yard chores.** Ask church members to nominate neighbors they know who could use a little help with summer lawn care or fall cleanups. After contacting them and discussing the need, send crews to get the work done. Make sure you've checked with the homeowner before removing trees or bushes or before using any chemicals or weed killers.

7. Gather accountants and tax preparers to **provide** for an evening at your church of **free tax advice for single**

parents. Make certain your helpers are qualified and prepared to talk about issues such as alimony, child support, child tax credits, budgeting, and separating taxes that were previously filed jointly. Advertise the service in the community events section of your local paper. This could grow into a monthly service.

6 Ways to Reach Families with Special Needs

1. **Provide training** for all Sunday school volunteers regarding special needs. Help teachers understand how to work effectively with kids with ADD, ADHD, autism, physical disabilities, emotional stress, etc. Organizations to provide quality help and training include your local school district, Center for Parent Information and Resources (parentcenterhub.org), or Abilities.com.

2. **Recruit buddies** who will adopt individual kids with special needs who come to church. Start with just one or two, and the word will quickly spread. Find a room with easy access and provide individual lessons for each of the kids. Ask the parents to provide as much information as they can that will be helpful in understanding and ministering to their child.

   Arrange for training for the volunteers focused on the needs of the first kids, provided by a local special-needs specialist. When new needs arise, bring the specialist back. If the kids are able, include them in the regular Sunday school classes along with their buddy for part of the time (*e.g.,* worship, game, lesson).

   Offer buddies for specially abled kids during regular outreach events such as VBS, AWANA, etc. Be sure to provide training for the buddies as well as the lead volunteers. Place the specially abled kids with care, taking into account the lead teacher and the other children. As always, make sure to provide adequate training.

3. **Provide a parent's night out** for parents of specially abled kids. Find volunteers who will come to the

house and babysit while the parent(s) go out. Raise the funds to provide the dinner and even an activity for the parent(s). If there's an adult event at the church, provide childcare so they can attend the event. Always provide training for the volunteers, provided through a local special-needs specialist.

4. Find a counselor who specializes in or has a heart for families with members who have special needs. **Provide** funding for parents to receive **counseling**.

5. **Adopt a family** with a specially abled child. Get to know them. Check in regularly through the medium they prefer (text, phone, or email). Ask for their prayer request and then pray faithfully for those requests. Drop off little gifts for the mom/dad/child with notes of encouragement. Visit the family regularly (every couple of weeks or once a month).

6. **Contact a local group home** that works with people with developmental disabilities. Work with the manager. Offer to either provide or reimburse the cost of weekly transportation to your church. Pay someone from the group home to train a group of volunteers from your church.

When these special guests arrive, treat them as local celebrities. Acknowledge them from the pulpit on their first day. Make sure seating is appropriate for them. Sit with them. Introduce them to your friends. Most of all, make sure they experience the love of Christ. Repeat every week. Recognize that this is a long-term commitment.

7 Ways to Reach Children

1. **Backyard Bible Clubs** are regular meetings at someone's home for neighbor children to come and learn about the Bible. Child Evangelism Fellowship (cefonline.com) has lots of resources for this. You can create your own as well. Make sure you have at least one other adult to help you. Include a Bible story, a craft, a game, and a snack. An hour is enough time, though you can go longer if you want.

2. Provide a **sports or fine arts camp** for a week during the summer. This is a great outreach opportunity requiring a fair amount of preparation. Recruit local high school/college students to oversee the sports/art. Start small (one or two sports or arts) so you can focus and do a quality job, and then add others in future years. Determine the time frame (half day is easier, but many kids won't be able to come). Include a Bible lesson, music, games, and competitions in addition to training in the sport/art. It's OK to charge, but work to keep it affordable for families in your neighborhood. Provide a way for parents to see what their child has learned (online videos they can access with a security code, or a performance at the end of the week).

3. Designate a **Bring a Friend to Church Day.** Suggest to parents that they host a sleepover the night before and then bring everyone to church. Make it a super-fun morning, full of prizes, quality teaching, good music, and encouragement to come back next week. Give parents tools to use to talk to their guest's parents about attending the upcoming weeks. Collect names and addresses and send postcards to the visitors during

the week. Offer incentives for returning the next week (*e.g.,* coupon for free donuts and coffee at the coffee shop, or prizes for the kids).

4. Offer **AWANA** (awana.org) **or a similar midweek club opportunity.** This requires a large time commitment from multiple volunteers, but kids learn Scripture, have fun, and make friends. Many families who won't come on Sunday find it OK to come during the week.

5. **Hold a kids carnival** on the church grounds or at a local park. Set up booths with games, activities, and art projects. Provide prizes and ice cream. Engage middle and high school students to man the booths in pairs. Keep the carnival to one or two hours for the sake of the volunteers. Keep the volunteers hydrated and fed. Provide simple bags with church information outside and inside for kids to collect their art and prizes.

6. **Host a Splash Day or Night** at the local rec center. Pay for kids to come swim and have fun one summer day. Promote it within and outside your church. Have church staff and volunteers available to talk with families as their kids play.

7. **Host Reach-Out Nights for Sunday school or VBS workers.** Provide names of visitor children, post cards or note paper, and stamps. Feed a snack or a pizza dinner to the workers to enjoy while they write follow-up notes to these families. Or provide phone numbers and have workers call these families with a friendly greeting, an offer to help with any needs, and information about upcoming family-oriented activities at the church.

10 Ways to Reach Youth

1. **Sponsor a place** near your local middle school or high school **to provide homework help and** a place **to hang out.** Provide snacks. Get to know the kids and provide encouragement. Offer prayers for their needs and concerns. Make sure there are always two adults present. This is a long-term commitment, so be prepared to stick with it for at least a full school year.

2. **Sponsor an event** at the local middle school or high school. Contact the school administration and ask for their recommendation and permission. Work closely with the school to follow their guidelines and needs. Take a genuine interest in the kids and provide generous food and encouragement.

3. **Adopt a middle school or high school student** in your neighborhood. Get to know them and their family. Look for ways to listen to them and encourage them. Ask for one way to pray for them and then follow up to see how things are going. Always include parents in whatever you do.

4. **Find a Christian organization** that reaches out to middle school or high school students in your area and ask them to identify a need you can fill. Fellowship of Christian Athletes (fca.org) and Cru (cru.org) (formerly known as Campus Crusade for Christ) are two such organizations.

5. **Contact the counselor at your local high school or middle school** to see if there are a couple of students

who could use some extra attention. Ask for permission to meet with them at the school, following whatever guidelines they set. Always bring another adult with you. Be willing to spend time getting to know your students and find ways to encourage them. Come with questions that show you're interested in learning about them and not judging them. Refrain from giving them money. Rather, give your time and attention. Earn their trust and look for ways to encourage them in their faith.

6. **Contact the local middle school and offer to invest in a club or school sports team** where you have an interest. If there isn't one that fits you, offer to start one with your gift or interest (*e.g.,* art, a language other than English, music, sewing, crafts, any sport, science, or leadership).

7. **Ask middle school or high school students to serve alongside you at a food bank or homeless shelter.** Be sure to obtain parental permission. Work out transportation with the parents. Observe the student's strengths and point them out. Remind them of Jesus' perspective on serving. Engage in spiritual conversations with them and affirm their spiritual growth through serving.

8. Find some athletic young adults to **play pick-up games** of basketball, volleyball, soccer, or whatever is appealing to students around you. Use your church grounds or a local park. Provide water and fruit or other snacks. Work on making it a regular occurrence.

Come prepared each week with something you've learned from God and look for a way to share that with one or more of the people who come.

9. **Find a Christian teacher** at your local middle school or high school. Meet with them to find out how you can support and encourage them. See if there is something they would want to initiate at the school with your help.

10. **Ask students to pray for their school with you.** Ask them what they think is important to God at their school. What are things to be thankful for? What are concerns? Pray at church or at the school.

7 Ways to Reach Local Schools and Their Staff

1. **Provide a meal for teachers.** You can pick the week they're preparing to open school, the day school gets out, during an in-service day, the day grades are due at the end of each term, just randomly, or when something difficult has happened in your community. Commit to one or more than one. Work with the administration to make sure you know how many teachers and provide well for them. Another option would be providing something thoughtful in each faculty and/or staff member's mailbox. Always include an appropriate blessing.

2. Offer to **help with after-school tutoring** of kids who need it. It could be just you or a group. This must be a weekly (or every other week) commitment for at least one school year.

3. **Adopt a classroom or a program at the school** that an administrator identifies as a need. Be sure to fill that need. Alternatively, adopt one or more teachers, having someone from the church personally attend to one teacher, kitchen worker, custodian, aide, or administrator. Get to know that person. Pray for them and leave them treats, encouraging notes, etc.

4. **Meet with the administrator and listen carefully to what he or she says about the needs of their school.** Pray about those needs and formulate a plan to meet one of the needs. Return to the administrator with your ideas and ask for their input and advice. Revise as necessary, then ask for permission to implement

the plan. Be sure you have obtained permission and blessing from the administration as well as your church.

5. Gather a group of prayer warriors to **pray weekly for one or more of the schools in your area**. Ask teachers and administrators for prayer requests if they're open to it.

6. Offer to **host a workday** with volunteers from your church to complete projects in the school the administration identifies: painting curbs and parking lines, cleaning up the school yard, washing windows, deep-cleaning bathrooms or classrooms during the summer or any break. Raise the funds to obtain the needed supplies. Be sure to obtain the supplies under the supervision of the school administration.

7. **Offer to help with ongoing volunteer tasks** that need to be done at the school: crossing guard, school ground clean-up, hall duty, classroom assistant, administrative assistance, pack snacks for food insecure students. Use an online sign-up tool such as sign-up genius (signupgenius.com) or doodle.com so you know who is helping when. Recruit someone to handle the administrative duties of overseeing the volunteers.

8 Ways to Reach Millennials

1. **Get to know some** – from work, the grocery store, the local artisan's show, or hair salon. Listen to them, ask their advice, and include God in your conversation when it's natural. Ask them questions about what they think about God and do not judge. Ask God for wisdom to ask more good questions and give thoughtful honest answers to their questions.

2. **Find a local cause** that attracts millennials and join it. Work alongside them and get to know them as you work. Always be ready to give an answer for your faith without being judgmental. Be ready, too, to ask questions of the millennials that will help them clarify their faith and lead toward God.

3. **Adopt an apartment complex** that houses millennials. Apartment Life (apartmentlife.org) is one place to start. Talk with the manager to obtain their permission. Ask the manager to help you design monthly activities that would appeal to the residents and do what they recommend. Be prepared to ask faith questions without forcing it.

4. **Hang out at a coffee shop** regularly and look for millennials. Slowly get to know one or two who are regulars. Look for ways to engage in a faith conversation.

5. **Partner with a ministry** that is effectively reaching millennials in your area such as Alpha (alphausa.org), Cru (cru.org), InterVarsity (intervarsity.org), or

Navigators (navigators.org). Fill a gap they have where you would fit well.

6. **Connect with the administration of a local community college, university, or trade school** to find out what need you could fill in service to their students. Figure out a way to fill that need.

7. **Open your home to students from a local college.** Work with the college to identify a student or small group of students who need a place to meet, perhaps to study or just to have a family. As you get to know them, include them in your family activities. Include your faith activities (prayer, faith discussions, Bible study, and church attendance) as you would normally.

8. **Host an art show** or dedicate a wall to art provided by millennials at your church. Ask them to oversee it if there's someone who stands out as an organizer. Recognize the artist and ask them to post something about their work near their submissions. Consider how you'll promote what you're doing as well as curate the submissions.

Some communities already have local art events (such as a First Friday Art Walk). If these are already in place in your town consider ways to participate.

6 Ways to Reach Seniors

1. **Create aid stations at local pickle ball courts.** Set up a booth near the area where players gather to talk and wait their turn to play. Provide sport drinks, snacks, towels, free sweat towels, water, and misters to cool down. You can generate greater interest by having a local expert at your booth or providing various demo paddles for seniors to borrow for free. Include a sign that says, "Free Pickle Ball Aid Station Compliments of Name of Your Church."

2. **Hold a health fair at your church.** Invite agencies and nonprofits in your community to set up booths focused on senior adult health. Contact your local hospital, mental health center, and gym or rec center to ask for services they can provide. Ask a nurse or doctor from your congregation to provide free vital signs screening. Don't forget to invite nutritionists, hearing specialists, and chiropractors as well. Local and national organizations that focus on cancer care, heart disease, and oral health may provide valuable help and resources for your outreach. Don't forget to set up a booth advertising the spiritual help your church provides.

3. **Create a grief care support group** at your church. Advertise the group in the local paper, on social media, and in magazines that target seniors. Griefshare.org offers curriculum and other valuable resources to help your church care for seniors (and others) who are working through grief.

4. **Create cancer care packages** you can take to the local cancer center. Talk with cancer survivors about things they needed. You'll find that lip balm, lotion, and puzzle books to pass the time will be in high demand. Include a devotional book and information about your church as well. If the cancer center won't allow you to deliver the baskets, just ask your congregation to nominate people they know who have been recently diagnosed.

5. **Set up in-home coffee breaks for shut-ins.** Make appointments and go in pairs. Take flavored coffee and cream and fresh pastries. Bring a candle or flowers to make your time together feel more like a morning out instead of in.

6. **Create weekly coffee shop discussion groups for seniors.** Establish one rule: no politics or complaining allowed. Each week provide a different discussion topic such as, "Why my grandkids are the best in the world," "Places I've visited that everyone should see," or "Three things I've done that would probably surprise you." If your local paper has a community events section, make sure you advertise your group there.

CHAPTER 8

OUTREACH SCRIPTURES TO KNOW AND USE

Gospel Message Explanations

The Romans Road

1. The Human Problem (Romans 3:10, Romans 3:23, and Romans 6:23). We're all sinful. Sin is anything that separates us from God, usually actions or words.

2. Humanity's Hope in Christ (Romans 5:8). God is our only hope.

3. The Sinner's Response (Romans 10:9, 10, 13) Call out to Jesus.

4. The Result of Salvation (Romans 5:1-2; 6:1-10; and Romans 8:1). Peace and hope—a new life!—comes to those who receive.

The Wordless Book (for children using the colors black, red, white, gold, and green)

Dark (black page): Romans 3:23. All of us have sinned. Sin is anything we think, do or say that doesn't please God. All sin has consequences.

Red: 1 Corinthians 15:3-5. God had a plan to cover the consequences. Jesus came to show us God's love. Jesus never sinned but died for our sins and then rose from the dead.

Clean (white page): John 1:12. When we choose to become God's child, we're cleaned from our sins. God sees us through "Jesus glasses."

Gold: John 14:2. We will live in Heaven (a perfect place) with God (who is perfect) forever.

Green: 1John 1:9. We are to grow in our faith by confessing our sins, reading God's Word, participating in God's church.

Scriptures to Know

Matthew 19: 25, 26

When the disciples heard this, they were greatly astonished and asked, "Who then can be saved?" Jesus looked at them and said, "With man this is impossible, but with God all things are possible."

Matthew 28:18-20

Then Jesus came to them and said, "All authority in heaven and on earth has been given to me. Therefore go and make disciples of all nations, baptizing them in the name of the Father and of the Son and of the Holy Spirit, and teaching them to obey everything I have commanded you. And surely I am with you always, to the very end of the age."

John 3:16-18

For God so loved the world that he gave his one and only Son, that whoever believes in him shall not perish but have eternal life. For God did not send his Son into the world to condemn the world, but to save the world through him. Whoever believes in him is not condemned, but whoever does not believe stands condemned already because they have not believed in the name of God's one and only Son.

John 5:24

"Very truly I tell you, whoever hears my word and believes him who sent me has eternal life and will not be judged but has crossed over from death to life."

John 14:1

"Do not let your hearts be troubled. You believe in God; believe also in me."

John 14:6

Jesus answered, "I am the way and the truth and the life. No one comes to the Father except through me."

Acts 2:38

Peter replied, "Repent and be baptized, every one of you, in the name of Jesus Christ for the forgiveness of your sins. And you will receive the gift of the Holy Spirit."

Acts 4:12

Salvation is found in no one else, for there is no other name under heaven given to mankind by which we must be saved.

Acts 16:30-34

"Sirs, what must I do to be saved?"

They replied, "Believe in the Lord Jesus, and you will be saved—you and your household." Then they spoke the word of the Lord to him and to all the others in his house. At that hour of the night the jailer took them and washed their wounds; then immediately he and all his household were baptized.

Romans 10:9, 10

If you declare with your mouth, "Jesus is Lord," and believe in your heart that God raised him from the dead, you will be saved. For it is with your heart that you believe and are justified, and it is with your mouth that you profess your faith and are saved.

2 Corinthians 5:21

God made him who had no sin to be sin for us, so that in him we might become the righteousness of God.

Ephesians 2:8, 9

For it is by grace you have been saved, through faith—and this is not from yourselves, it is the gift of God—not by works, so that no one can boast.

Galatians 3:26, 27

In Christ Jesus you are all children of God through faith, for all of you who were baptized into Christ have clothed yourselves with Christ.

Hebrews 7:25

Therefore he is able to save completely those who come to God through him, because he always lives to intercede for them.

1 Peter 3:15, 16

But in your hearts revere Christ as Lord. Always be prepared to give an answer to everyone who asks you to give the reason for the hope that you have. But do this with gentleness and respect, keeping a clear conscience, so that those who speak maliciously against your good behavior in Christ may be ashamed of their slander.

Revelation 3:20

Here I am! I stand at the door and knock. If anyone hears my voice and opens the door, I will come in and eat with that person, and they with me.

CHAPTER 9

OUTREACH PRAYERS

Helpful Guidelines
- Pray in the moment. Praying later is also fine, but pray with the person before you part company.
- Be specific, simple, and short.
- Avoid *Christianese*. Use common words that everyone will understand.
- Don't make God a genie in a bottle who grants wishes, or a dictator who has certain expectations or standards to be met.
- Start your prayers by stating what you know about God that's important to your prayer.
- End by giving God the glory.

Special Situations

When a person is ready to accept Christ as Lord, it's best for him or her to do the praying. Ask them to pray aloud so if they get stuck or are unsure, you can help them. Make sure they include these few key ideas: I'm a sinner; I believe in Jesus (his life, death and resurrection), and I want to commit to following Jesus.

If you're praying with someone about a worry or fear, try something like this: "Father God, you know everything and control everything. You created all things and love all your creation. My friend, ____, is worried about _____. You have told us not to worry, but we still do. Help ____ understand your presence with them. Speak to ____ about your love for them. Give them wisdom to see ____ (this situation) through your eyes. Give ____ courage to face what lies ahead. We will trust you to see this through and provide what's best for ____. In Jesus' name, Amen."

If you're praying with someone about a situation at work, try something like this: "Father God, you are all-knowing and wiser than we are. You are never taken by surprise. You care about ____ and ____ (the situation). Please give ____ the wisdom and understanding to see more clearly what is involved in ____ (the situation). Help ____ to perceive things that might have been missed. Give ____ the courage to do what is right. Remind ____ of your loving kindness toward them. We will trust you and wait for you to lead. In Jesus' name, Amen."

If you're praying for a specific need, try something like this: "Father God, you know each of us, including our needs and wants. You know what is best for us. You know ____ so well. You know ____'s needs, especially for ____ (the need). We're asking you to help ____ with ____ (the need). Remind ____ of your great love for him/her. We acknowledge our limitations and don't know how to solve this need. So, we'll wait for you to show ____ the way you want him/her to go. We will trust you and wait for you. In Jesus' name, Amen."

CHAPTER 10

SIMPLE WAYS TO SHARE YOUR FAITH

*N*o two situations are the same when it comes to sharing your faith, so there can be no single prepared speech or example. There are a few keys to remember.

- Always be "prayed up." You won't have the right words to say or notice the right person without God's leading.
- Don't force a conversation. Wait for natural opportunities to share the hope you have.
- Always be prepared to have more than one conversation with the person you meet. God works through relationships, not one-time encounters.
- Look beyond your needs and interests to see the needs of those God puts in your path.
- Don't make assumptions about the people you talk with. God may give you a revelation, but most likely not. Assume only that they're fellow human beings.
- Always be willing to give an explanation for the hope and joy you have.
- Always be willing to ask the person you're talking with to make a commitment to

talk with God about their faith (or lack thereof).

- Refrain from lecturing or preaching. Neither will change another's mind.
- Include God in your everyday conversation as often as it is natural.
- Ask God to show you one person you're supposed to reach out to. Watch expectantly and listen carefully to the Holy Spirit's leading regarding what to say.

If you're talking with someone you just met in a **social setting**, find something you have in common. Is it children or neighborhood or hobby or music preference? Ask questions till you find your commonality, then build a bond based on that. Express sincere interest in their opinions and ideas. When it's appropriate, share how God has worked in or through your common interest. Do not force it. If the opportunity doesn't present itself in your first conversation, look for a way to continue your conversation in the near future.

If you're reaching out to people in the **service industry**, ask for one thing you can pray for on their behalf. Pray for them in that moment if it's appropriate. Also pray consistently once you part. Then return to find them and ask how that one thing is going. Tell them how you've been praying for them. Express a sincere interest in them. Tell them what you know about how God answers prayers. Return as often as you can, checking in with them. Encourage them to pray as well. Rejoice when the prayers are answered. Share with them how God knows them and cares for them.

If you're talking with a **neighbor or co-worker,** ask them about what they believe about God. Be willing to listen and ask clarifying, nonjudgmental questions. If they're open, share what you believe regarding one of the things they brought up. Look for ways your beliefs are similar to what they believe. Explain differences without being judgmental or argumentative. Ask them if they would be willing to continue the conversation soon. Offer to buy a co-worker lunch or coffee to talk more. Invite a neighbor to your house for the continuation of your conversation.

With anyone, look for chances to **talk about a specific way God is working in your life** without being dramatic or forcing the topic. Be honest about your feelings and experience. Don't make it overly involved and keep it simple. Do this often, as a natural part of your conversations.

Invite a neighbor or co-worker to a church-sponsored event or church service. If they choose to go with you, make them, not your friends, the focus of your attention. Don't treat them as show and tell. Make sure you explain things that may be confusing to them or make them feel awkward. For example, if there are times where everyone stands or sits, be sure to let them know ahead of time. Be sure they know what sort of things to wear or not wear. (Is it super-casual, business casual, or anything goes?) Be aware of how they're feeling and what things they may want to talk about. Spend time with them afterwards debriefing the experience and answering questions.

CHAPTER 11

BUILDING RELATIONSHIPS

*B*uilding relationships is the most important step to reaching any community for Christ. It takes time and commitment. It requires listening before speaking. It necessitates asking questions before making recommendations. It involves patience and being honest. It entails doing your homework to be prepared with a Biblical answer for the hope you have. It demands that we live our faith before we preach it. It compels us to realize that others may know better than we do about what is needed. It forces us to put aside our agendas so we can hear more clearly. It demands patience, lots of it. It expects the Holy Spirit to lead and guide.

Tips to remember when building relationships.

- We should never diminish or neglect our faith. The goal is to build a relationship based on faith, regardless of where it starts.

- There can be no relationship without trust and honesty.

- Listen first and long. Ask clarifying questions and repeat back what you've heard until the person can say, "Yes, that's it!"

- Don't build a relationship just so you can convert them. Build the relationship so you can love them.

- Live your faith before you speak it.
- Put aside all agendas. Be willing to be vulnerable about your feelings, issues, and life.
- Ask for advice or other forms of help. Borrow something from them or ask them to teach you how to do something.
- Don't assume you're always right. Be open-minded.
- Honor their communication preferences. Some prefer texts while others want a phone call. Some prefer email while others like a knock on the door.
- Be prepared with Biblical examples for the hope you have, but don't insist on using one in every encounter.
- Remember that God alone brings someone to faith in Christ. Be his hands and feet. Be his voice but try not to be in the way.
- Try putting yourself in the other person's shoes and looking through their eyes. Their experiences may be foreign to you, so ask them to help you understand.
- Remember: you are not the Savior; Jesus is. We are not superior to our neighbor or co-worker. They most likely have some very valuable things to teach us.
- We need to be aware that some of our good intentions could be harmful if we don't listen well.
- We need to understand that every person has their own culture because of where

they grew up, what they've experienced, and the way God made them. Our culture is no better or worse than anyone else's. We cannot fully understand theirs, but we need to accept that theirs is valid and real. We need to be sure we're honoring their culture even when we don't agree with it. It means we can grow and be more beautiful by learning from others just as they can grow and be more beautiful by learning from us.

CHAPTER 12

DISCUSSION QUESTIONS

*C*hoose from these questions something to discuss with your team as you prepare for or reflect on the outreach project(s) you're tackling together.

To Discuss Anytime

1. Which of the five contrasts in Chapter 1 is newest to you? Most challenging to you? Least understandable? Explain why.

2. In your own words, explain the difference between a spiritual outreach project (one initiated by Christians) and a purely secular outreach project (one initiated by a business or service organization not connected with the church). Do you believe you can make spiritual impact by participating in the latter? Why or why not?

3. React to this sentence from Chapter 2: "The church does not have a mission; God's mission has the church." What do you understand this to mean? How does it affect your team's perspective on your project?

4. Reflect on this principle from Chapter 2: "Effective outreach is not a program, but a posture." To what degree would you say outreach is the posture of your congregation? To what degree is outreach the posture of your life? What one step could you or your church take to make outreach a higher priority?

5. Which of the Scriptures in Chapter 3 do you most want to remember as you participate in your outreach project? Why?

6. Why is faithfulness only to church programs and people not enough if we're to reach non-Christians with the gospel?

7. What have you learned from past efforts to reach non-Christians with the gospel?

8. For each person on your team, identify a talent or temperament quality or spiritual gift you have observed that equips them perfectly for a role in your outreach project.

9. Survey the summary of outreach activities in Chapter 5 and the list of 121 specific ideas in Chapter 7. Choose two to four from these lists that interest you most and tell your group why.

To Discuss Before Your Outreach Project

1. Which of the five principles in Chapter 2 will best be demonstrated by your project? Which of them do you find most challenging or intimidating? Which motivates you most?

2. What prayer request do you have for yourself before you begin? What prayer request do you have for those you'll be serving?

To Discuss After Your Outreach Project

1. Tell your group about one person you met as you served. What is their story? What spiritual needs did you hear from them or discern in your conversation with them?

2. What surprised you about what you experienced? What challenged you? What did you find most gratifying?

3. How do you believe God used you and will use what you accomplished? How will you pray about that? Why is it important to you to know how he answers?

CHAPTER 13

OUTREACH ORGANIZATIONS
AND MINISTRIES

Outreach (outreach.com) has something for every ministry, loads of training, ideas, resources, and more.

Apartment Life (apartmentlife.org) is a Christian organization that reaches out to people living in apartment complexes across the country.

Billy Graham Evangelistic Association/The Billy Graham Center (billygraham.org) contains a variety of resources for reaching out to others in all kinds of situations.

Cru, formerly known as **Campus Crusade** (cru.org) has plenty of resources for college students.

Christ In Youth (ciy.com) offers high-quality conferences and experiences as well as international mission trips for preteens through high school students across the country.

City Gospel Movements (citygospelmovements.org) is a network of ministries and people who want to reach cities for Christ. Their website is full of information, coaching, and inspiration.

Coalition for Christian Outreach (ccojubilee.org) is dedicated to reaching college students and connecting them to local churches.

Dare2Share (dare2sharelive.com) has resources and conferences for students.

Global Outreach Missions/Mission Go (missiongo.org) has been training and sending missionaries for 75 years.

Institute for Cross-Cultural Mission (gracedc.institute) has amazing resources to help churches understand cultural differences and welcome everyone as Christ welcomes us.

Love INC/Love In the Name of Christ (loveinc.org) is a nationwide organization that mobilizes and unites churches to transform lives in their communities.

Luis Palau Association (palau.org) provides wonderful evangelistic information, resources, and events around the world.

Navigators (navigators.org) has tons of resources for college and young adult ministry.

The Source for Youth Ministry (thesource4ym.com) has lots of very helpful ideas, free training videos, and articles for reaching out to youth.

Youthministry.com (Group) has articles, podcasts, blogs, and tons of resources.

Youth with a Mission/YWAM (ywam.org) is a worldwide outreach, training young men and women for mission.

CHAPTER 14

RECOMMENDED RESOURCES

Programs and Courses
Outreach.com can help you find speakers and performers (events), movies that share God's love (films), books of all kinds related to outreach (resources), and supplies to tell others what you're doing (marketing).

Outreach New Mover Plus: a program through Outreach, Inc., that automatically sends a postcard invitation from your church to everyone who moves into your neighborhood.

Alpha (alphausa.org) is an evangelistic course that introduces the basics of the Christian faith through a series of open and honest talks and discussions.

Crown Financial (crown.org) is a Christian nonprofit that helps people improve their finances and promotes stewardship values all over the world.

Discovery Bible Study is an approach used in many countries to help everyday Christians study the Bible, including Bible studies with those still coming to faith. A Google search for "Discovery Bible Study" will yield a long list of possible resources, including discoverapp.org/discovery-bible-study.

DivorceCare (divorcecare.org) is a Biblical, Christ-centered divorce support group ministry. Their resources help equip a lay-led team for effective and ongoing divorce ministry.

Financial Peace University (daveramsey.org) teaches how money need not be stressful. The classes teach sound financial strategies to get out of debt and stay that way.

Re-engage (marriagehelp.org) is a safe way for couples to move forward in their marriages, whether they rate their relationship as a 2 or a 10.

The Marriage Course (themarriagecourse.org) is based on Christian principles but designed for all couples with or without a church background.

Verge (vergenetwork.org) equips anyone for mission within the context of community.

Books and Other Printed Resources
Outreach Magazine is a bimonthly magazine full of information, practical resources, and encouragement.

The Case for Christ by Lee Strobel is a concise explanation for Christ's deity and the need for faith in him from a journalist who did not believe, but came to faith by investigating the claims of Christianity. It comes in versions for adults, youth, and children.

Cold-Case Christianity by J. Warner Wallace is the result of an atheist homicide detective's work to disprove the Biblical claims of Jesus' death and resurrection. Also available in a kid's version.

Conspiracy of Kindness by Steve Sjogren describes how to demonstrate God's love in practical ways.

Eats with Sinners by Arron Chambers contains practical ideas and questions to use while eating with your friends who don't know Jesus.

Evidence That Demands a Verdict by Josh McDowell is a classic that delineates all of the evidence for God, Jesus, and the Bible. An updated and expanded version is available.

Finish the Mission by John Piper (and a host of well-known outreach gurus) gives fresh insight into the Great Commission.

The Gospel Primer by Caesar Kalinowski is designed to help any group of people cultivate a practical understanding of the gospel and grow in gospel fluency, the ability to proclaim and demonstrate the gospel in absolutely every area of life.

Jill's House: The Gift of Rest is a great resource for learning about how your church can reach out to children with special needs and their families (available at churchleaders. com).

The Language of God: A Scientist Presents Evidence for Faith by Francis S. Collins recounts the author's personal struggle with doubt and shows how his commitment to science reconciles with his belief in God.

The Master Plan for Evangelism by Robert Coleman is a timeless book that explains how to minister to those God puts in our lives.

Mere Christianity by C. S. Lewis. The classic apologetic for the Christian faith.

More than a Carpenter by Josh McDowell is a classic, debating whether Jesus is a lunatic, a liar, or the Lord. An updated version is also available.

Organic Outreach by Kevin Harney offers help for sharing your faith in simple ways.

The Reason for God by Tim Keller addresses fears and doubts of nonbelievers and believers alike and presents rational reasoning for God.

Spiritual Parenting is about learning to create a home environment conducive to shaping the hearts and minds of children. Also, see the six-part video series available at Right Now Media (rightnowmedia.org).

The Unsaved Christian: Reaching Cultural Christians With the Gospel by Dean Inserra describes different types of nominal Christians along with ways to engage them.

Unlikely Converts by Randy Newman gives surprising faith stories and practical ways to proclaim the gospel even to those you'd least expect to accept it.

You Found Me by Rick Richardson provides new research on how those outside the church are surprisingly open to faith.

WOW! The Good News in Four Words by Dandi Daley Mackall is a fabulous book for preschool and early elementary kids that clearly and simply explains the gospel message.

ABOUT THE CONTRIBUTORS

Mark A. Taylor has served in a variety of editorial, marketing, and management roles in a Christian publishing career that spanned more than 40 years, including 14 years as editor and publisher of *Christian Standard* magazine. Now retired, Mark continues to take on a variety of editing and writing tasks as well as traveling, gardening, teaching, and serving in his local church.

Karl Leuthauser serves as the senior leader of Grace Community Church in southwestern Colorado. He previously spent a decade in Christian publishing where he served as an editor and executive. He has contributed to a large and wide variety of Bible studies and other resources for churches and has ghostwritten for Tony Dungy and Kyle Petty. He is married with four daughters and has a passion for backpacking in the deep woods of the rugged San Juan Mountains.

Heather Dunn has been involved in children's ministry since the age of twelve and has loved working in small, medium, and large churches. She has also written and edited for a number of Christian publishers. But most of all, she loves Jesus and helping to spread the Good News! She's also pretty crazy about her husband, two wonderful children, and her grandchildren.

And with special gratitude...
We're indebted to the following Christian leaders and outreach champions for their gracious willingness to share their wisdom and stories. Their expertise, insight, passion, and experience helped make this book the rich resource it is.

Steve Bond, lead pastor, Summit Christian Church, Sparks, Nevada

Ben Cachiaras, lead pastor, Mountain Christian Church, Joppa, Maryland

Arron Chambers, lead pastor, Journey Christian Church, Greeley, Colorado

David Dummitt, senior pastor, Willow Creek Community Church, South Barrington, Illinois

Glen Elliott, lead pastor, Pantano Christian Church, Tucson, Arizona

Brian Jennings, lead minister, Highland Park church, Tulsa, Oklahoma

Jennifer Reed, outreach and involvement minister, Mount Gilead Christian Church, Mooresville, Indiana

Names   Phone and Email

_____   _____

_____   _____

_____   _____

_____   _____

_____   _____

_____   _____

_____   _____

_____   _____

_____   _____